PHILOSOPHIC TURNINGS

Essays in Conceptual Appreciation

Philosophic Turnings

ESSAYS IN CONCEPTUAL APPRECIATION

By PAUL ZIFF

CORNELL UNIVERSITY PRESS

Ithaca, New York

CORNELL UNIVERSITY PRESS

First published 1966

Second printing 1967

701

Z68

BH 41

Z5

Library of Congress Catalog Card Number: 66-23406

PRINTED AND BOUND IN THE UNITED STATES OF AMERICA
BY VALLEY OFFSET, INC.
BOUND BY VAIL-BALLOU PRESS, INC.

In Memory Of
Pauline Pitkorchemna Ziff

Preface

FOR the time being, the only way to stick to the point in philosophy is to wander: any question is coiled around another; a winding path is followed. These essays represent the various turns I have taken in the past fifteen years.

Art, words, and minds are the main topics touched on. The attempt is always the same: to appreciate our conceptual situation. But since we are in dark ages, appreciation is at best partial, incomplete, for the time being.

PAUL ZIFF

University of Wisconsin
June 1966

Contents

PHILOSOPHIC TURNINGS

Essays in Conceptual Appreciation

in vain, in vain, in vain.
I am Henry Pussy-cat! My whiskers fly.

JOHN BERRYMAN
77 Dream Songs

I

Art and the
"Object of Art"*

A PERSISTENT myth in present day aesthetics is the
myth that when we discuss a work of art we are talking
about some "illusory" or "imaginary" thing sometimes
called the "object of art" or the "aesthetic object." I can
explain this by quoting Samuel Alexander.

More than once I have pointed out how in the beautiful object
the significance is supplied in part from the artist's mind; how
it is he who makes the flat Madonna seem, as Mr. Berenson
puts it, a tangible three-dimensional being, or who gives divine
playfulness to the Hermes, or motion and dance to the motion-
less maidens in the picture of the Spring, or who finds the
perfect, the only fitting word, to express a meaning that springs
from him, . . . And I have contrasted the object of art with
the mere percept where also half comes from the perceiver's
mind and half from what he directly sees: the coloured
moving shape is perceived to be a man, though sight alone
without memory does not say so. The contrast . . . is this: the
characters we impute to the object perceived, if we perceive
correctly, really do belong to the object and may be sensed

* Revised from an essay originally published in *Mind*, LX
(1951); reprinted by permission.

there on proper occasion; the coloured shape is the visible surface of a man; but in the work of art there is always illusion: the Hermes is not divine but only seems so, and the girls in the Spring are not in motion. At the same time, I have added, the artistic illusion is unlike ordinary perceptual illusion, for that illusion disappears to better acquaintance, is recognized to be an illusion. Whereas the illusion is of the essence of the work of art—ceases, therefore, to be illusion and makes the object significant.[1]

Take a particular example, a Cezanne still-life of some apples. In describing Cezanne's painting we may say 'The apples are solid, round full-volumes—like tangible three-dimensional things. The painting has great depth.' But that painting is a thin strip of canvas covered with bits of pigment. The canvas is flat, but the work of art has great depth? So Alexander arrives at the view that the work of art is distinct from the painting; the characters we impute to the painting do not really belong to it. We speak of solid voluminous apples, but there are only bits of pigment on the surface of the canvas. Thus there is an illusion, and this illusion is the object of art, that which we call beautiful, that which we judge, criticize, evaluate, and in general, discuss. It is as simple as this.

Alexander is not the only aesthetician to have adopted such a view. For analogous reasons Collingwood has claimed that the work of art is an "imaginary object." In a similar vein, S. C. Pepper contends that the work of art is our "perceptions" of the painting. De Witt Parker, following Bosanquet, held similar views. Not all these aestheticians agree that there is an illusion involved in our perception of a painting, but they all maintain, along with Alexander, that there is a significant discrepancy between the painting and the work of art; they agree with Alexander in claiming that the characters we impute to the painting do not really belong to the painting, but rather, are charac-

[1] *Philosophical and Literary Pieces*, p. 259.

2

ters of the work of art. Just what the work of art is held to be varies from one philosopher to another: for Collingwood it is an "imaginary object"; Pepper contends that it is a "series of intermittent perceptions"; Alexander insists it is an "illusion"; and so forth. But all agree that the painting is not the work of art. The prevalent opinion in aesthetics today seems to be in general accordance with Alexander's account. This is why it is important to show that his view is mistaken.

I

First of all we must consider the notion that there is an illusion involved in observing a painting. This particular point is somewhat peculiar to Alexander. Although other aestheticians claim there is a discrepancy between the characters we impute to the painting and the characters it actually possesses, few are prepared to maintain that there is any illusion at work here. Thus, even though I may succeed in dispelling the illusion that there is illusion involved in observing a painting, I shall not have dispelled the illusion that there is some discrepancy between the characters we impute to the painting and the characters the painting actually possesses. Nonetheless, it is fruitful to begin our discussion by pointing out that all talk of illusion is mistaken; although it does not follow from the fact that there is no illusion at work here that the characters we impute to the painting really do belong to the painting, it would follow from the fact—if it were a fact—that there is an illusion at work here that the characters we impute to the painting do not really belong to the painting. Thus it is important to show that there is no illusion at work here, even though showing this does not prove all that we want to prove. To show that all talk of illusion is mistaken we must be clear about what is meant in speaking of an illusion.

A traveller crossing a desert may suddenly see a lake

spread out before him; he stares at it, rubs his eyes, looks again; the waters beckon; he rushes forward, plunges his hand into hot sand. He was the victim of a mirage—an illusion. He thought there was water there, it looked like water, but it was only sand. This is one example of what an illusion is like. Suppose someone suffers from hallucinations, sees an illusory apple on the table before him. He thinks an apple is there, he sees an apple, but when he reaches out to grasp it, there is nothing to be grasped. He is deceived, he too is the victim of an illusion. Mirages and hallucinations are two types of visual illusions. There are others still more common. But there are other things which are sometimes spoken of as "illusions" which are not illusions at all. For example, if we asked someone to describe what he sees when he looks at railroad tracks he might say 'They look as if they converge in the distance.' We are familiar with this sort of description of railroad tracks. If anyone said this we should not feel anything wrong with what he was saying; in a way, they do look as if they converge, even though we know that they do not. One can look long and hard at railroad tracks, squint, peer off into the distance, but they still look as if they converge, even though they do not in fact converge. But, ordinarily, there is nothing illusory about looking at railroad tracks; no one is deceived. If a child, say, were to look at the railroad tracks and ask 'How do the trains run on the tracks when they come together?' in such a case we would feel inclined to speak of an illusion. This point can, perhaps, be made clear by considering the matter in a slightly different fashion. Suppose a prankster laid out some railroad tracks which, instead of running parallel to one another, diverged in such a manner as to make them look parallel. Would anyone who stood at the right point on the tracks and looked off into the distance say 'The tracks look as if they run parallel' ? Someone could describe what he saw in that way, but, most likely, he would be too amazed to say anything at all: he would think he was suffering from an illusion. But suppose he said to someone who was not looking at these queer tracks 'The tracks look as if they run parallel to one another.' The person who heard this would, most likely, not be the least astonished; a railroad foreman could ask one of his crew to take a look at the tracks they had just laid to see if they were parallel. He might then be told 'The tracks look as if they run parallel,' and such a response would not be apt to make him stare in amazement. We can and do describe what we see when we look at ordinary railroad tracks by saying either 'The tracks look as if they run parallel' or 'The tracks look as if they converge.' We should not ordinarily say that either description is the report of an illusion; whether or not we say a particular description is the report of an illusion depends on whether the person who gives the description of what he sees is likely to be deceived or not.

Now consider what happens when we look at a painting, and whether there is anything in such a situation which can properly be spoken of as an illusion. Suppose, while looking at a Cezanne still-life, we say 'It has great depth. The apples pictured are full, solid volumes.' This is the kind of thing we may say when, for instance, we are in a gallery discussing the painting. In saying this I do not wish to suggest that we are apt to say this only in such a situation, for this is not true. There are many situations, many different ones, in which we may say exactly the same thing. All I wish to suggest is that at least one of the situations where we may say such a thing is the one I have just mentioned. When we are in the painting gallery discussing the painting, and when we say 'The painting has great depth,' are we deceived into believing that we could walk through the canvas, put our hands in it, move around inside? Does the canvas look as though we could walk into and through it? The canvas looks as though it has great depth? Another way of putting this question is to ask: does the frame around the painting look, say, like the frame of an open window? Or like a doorway through which we could pass freely? We often do say that a painting is much like a window; a window through which we can see all kinds of strange and fascinating things which cannot be seen through any ordinary window. When we see an ordinary open window it really does look as though we can pass through the window. But when we see a painting which we sometimes speak of as a window through which to view the world, it does not really look as though we could pass our hands and feet through it. Not at all. The canvas looks flat just as it is flat. Are we to suppose when Alexander first saw the "flat Madonna" he speaks of, that he could not see that the picture of the Madonna was painted on a flat canvas?—that the painted canvas did not look flat to him? Did he have to go up and look closely at the canvas to see that it actually was flat, and that it would be futile for him to attempt to clamber through? This seems unlikely. The only type of painting where the canvas does not look flat is what we call a work of *"trompe l'oeil"*—and the name is tailor-made; it is a type of painting where the artist has amused himself, and possibly his audience, by creating optical illusions. When we first look at this sort of work we may be deceived and fail to realize that we are looking at a painting. In observing a work of *trompe l'oeil* we are apt to suppose that the picture of an apple is not a picture but a real apple. The apple looks as though we could take it in our hands. And people sometimes are deceived. Just as children might be deceived by the "illusion" of railroad tracks converging and might have to be taken for a walk along the tracks to be convinced that they do not in fact converge, so people sometimes must touch the canvas, must peer at it, to convince themselves that the picture of an apple is indeed just that, not a real apple after all. But neither Cezanne's paintings nor the Renaissance Madonnas are works of *trompe l'oeil*. If Alexander was correct in claiming that "the illusion is of the essence of the work of art" and if this kind of illusion is the kind he is talking about then there would be no way of distinguishing a work of *trompe l'oeil* from any other work—but in fact we do make such a distinction. (It is true that it is hard to draw a clear cut line between those works which are properly spoken of as works of *trompe l'oeil* and those which are not; here, as everywhere, there are borderline cases. Red merges imperceptibly into blue—but who would on that account say that red is blue?) It is true that there are paintings which produce optical illusions, and the fact that they do is adequately indicated by the way we label them. In calling them works of *"trompe l'oeil"* we indicate that these paintings do deceive the eye, and in this respect are unlike other paintings which are not works of *trompe l'oeil*. Thus it is true to say that there are some paintings which produce optical illusions, and if this was what Alexander was saying then he would be correct. However, it is obvious that this is not what Alexander was saying. I take it that when he says "the illusion is of the essence of the work of art," he is saying that every work of art has something to do with an illusion and not merely that there are some works of art which have something to do with an illusion. Unless we are prepared to maintain the false view that all paintings are works of *trompe l'oeil*, and not merely that some are, we have, as yet, seen no evidence which would warrant Alexander's statement that "the illusion is of the essence of the work of art." And we must note that even though there are some paintings which have something to do with an illusion, these paintings are relatively few in number, indeed, quite scarce, and they are of slight interest to the aesthetician. By far the greatest number of paintings are, in this respect, like Cezanne's canvases. The canvases are flat and they appear flat, they are seen as flat, they look flat. No one is ever deceived.

We have seen that one important characteristic of illu-

7

sions is not applicable to paintings. This is the fact that we are deceived by illusions, but we are not deceived by any ordinary painting. This is, in itself, sufficient to indicate that all talk of illusion is misleading. But we need not stop here, for, as we press the matter, it becomes more and more apparent that there can be no question of an illusion. A person on the desert might be familiar with mirages and thus might not be deceived by what he sees. Thus, in this case, looking at the painting might be analogous to looking at the mirage, for in neither case is there any deception. But the similarity between the two cases begins and ends at this point. No one has to study the mirage, examine and grow familiar with it before he says 'It looks as if there is a lake in the distance.' A single glance will suffice to reveal the lake in the distance. But this is totally unlike what occurs when people look at a Cezanne painting. It may take some time to see the depth in one of his paintings; the observer must first grow familiar with the painting, get to know it by carefully examining the structure, composition, design, and so forth. Of course, there are many paintings which do not require such extensive study. For example, even a quick look at Rembrandt's "Night Watch" will suffice to show that it is a picture of a group of figures, some in front of others. But there are many paintings for which a brief glance will not suffice to disclose the volumes and spaces and, with such a painting, we must first get to know it before we can see its depth. An analogy with music may be useful here. This process of getting to know a painting has its counterpart in the process of getting to know a piece of music. When we first hear a somewhat complex work, say a Bach violin partita, we may have difficulty in recognizing the themes and in following the variations. When we do know the work we can then hear the themes clearly. Can we say that this process of getting to know a work of art is the progressive growth of an illusion? If to see the volumes and space in a painting is to have an illusion then it seems we should describe this process of getting to know a painting as the progressive growth of an illusion, the deliberate cultivation of an hallucination. But if this is an illusion it is unlike anything else which we ordinarily call an illusion. It is so unlike anything which is ordinarily called an illusion that it seems grotesque to speak of it in this way. Finally, after having managed to see the depth in a Cezanne painting, we can often revert to our original way of seeing it. That is, sometimes we can choose to see it as having depth or to see it as flat. Who can do this with an illusion? The illusion of the lake in the distance is not something that can be dispelled at will. And the same thing is true of all illusions. But this is totally unlike the so-called "illusion" of space in the Cezanne still-life. In looking at a Cezanne still-life we can often choose either to see the painting as flat or to see it as having depth.

So far I have failed to turn up any evidence for Alexander's statement "the illusion is of the essence of the work of art." But I cannot leave the matter like this. For, from what has so far been said, it would seem that Alexander was an utterly confused thinker and had not the slightest idea of what an illusion was like. And this is not true. I think Alexander is mistaken in what he says, but I do not think it is a foolish or a naive mistake. If I cannot present what he is saying in a more plausible light, this only points to a failure in my analysis. However, I think I can make his position seem plausible if I approach it in a certain manner. It was mentioned above that we often do say a painting is much like a window. And I argued that looking at a painting is, except perhaps with works of *trompe l'oeil*, not at all like looking at an open window. I still believe that what I said is true. But I failed to point out that looking at a painting may seem much like looking at a closed window, and it may also seem much like looking through a closed window. For example, someone standing before a closed window may look through the glass at, say, the landscape outside. But he may also look at the glass of the window. Similarly, someone standing before a painting may look, as it were, through the canvas and see a new and fascinating landscape. But he may also look at the canvas. When we look at a closed window, especially if the glass is somewhat dusty, we do not think we can pass through the window, for we know quite well that the glass will prevent us from doing this. It does not look as though we could actually pass through the glass, and the only time it would look that way is when the window looks just like an open window. Nonetheless, we can look through the glass, and we know that what we see is on the other side of the glass. Thus looking at a painting seems much like looking at a somewhat dusty window. But when we look through the canvas we know that what we see is not on the other side of the canvas. For what we see when we look through the canvas is no-where and no-when. The canvas looks as though there is something beyond it, but in fact there is nothing. Thus there is an illusion. When we look through a window we look at, say, the landscape. But when we look through the canvas we look at the aesthetic object, the work of art. Thus the work of art is akin to the Red Queen in that it too exists only on the other side of the glass. And this is a persuasive picture of what occurs when we look at paintings.

But even though this account is persuasive when looked at in one way, if we approach it with a critical eye its persuasiveness can be dispelled. For, in fact, looking through a canvas is quite unlike looking through a glass, and this despite the fact that an analogy can be made out between them. When we look through a glass—even a dusty one— it does look as though we could walk around in the space beyond the glass, as though there is a place for head and hands and feet on the other side of the glass. But when we look through a canvas it does not look at all like this. The only time it would look like this is when we look at works of *trompe l'oeil*. And I have already pointed out that these are special and rare cases. If when we looked through what we took to be a window, even a dusty window, we found that there was nothing outside, no other side to the glass, we should be astounded. In such a case I assume that it did look as though there was something on the other side of the glass. It would be like looking across the room through a dusty window at what we took to be the house across the street only to find that some astounding artist had painted the whole scene on our window pane. In such a case it really would look as though there was something on the other side of the glass. But this is not at all like what does happen when we look at an ordinary painting, or even when we look through an ordinary painting. And it is no good saying that if we put the painting in the window frame in place of the glass and if we arranged the lighting in a certain way and if we then had a person look at it who did not know what had been done, then it would look to him as though there was something on the other side of the painting. For all this is to say no more than that if the painting did not look the way it does in fact ordinarily look, then it might look as though there was something on the other side of the painting. Perhaps we could play such tricks with paintings, but whether it could be done or not is totally irrelevant to what I am saying. In saying that when we look through a painting it does not look as though there is something on the other side of the painting, I am not talking about what might be the case. I am talking only about what is the case, and the fact that something else might be the case does not in the least matter.

Thus, I repeat, we have not as yet seen any evidence which would warrant Alexander's statement that "the illusion is of the essence of the work of art." Perhaps this is owing to the fact that, as Alexander states, "the artistic illusion is unlike ordinary perceptual illusion." And we must admit that it is unlike ordinary perceptual illusion, much unlike it. Indeed, so much unlike anything we ordinarily speak of as an illusion that, as yet, we have not seen the slightest reason for speaking of it as an illusion. However, I need not further labor this point. It is clear that Alexander did think something queer was going on and he used the word 'illusion' to describe it. One of the things that he, along with some other aestheticians, finds queer is the way we ordinarily talk about paintings. Here we have the real question.

II

The real question before us is, to use Alexander's terms, whether the characters we impute to a painting really do belong to the painting or not. Alexander, along with some other aestheticians, claims that they do not. Thus they claim that we often say things about paintings which are not in fact true of the paintings. Of course, they do not claim that none of the things we say about paintings are in fact true of the paintings, but only that some of the things we say about paintings are not in fact true. And what is more, it is the important and interesting things we say about paintings that are not in fact true. For example, such statements as 'The painting has great depth,' 'The apples pictured are full of solid volumes,' are held to be not in fact true. It is not too difficult to see one reason why they are inclined to say this. There are times when we point to a painting by Cezanne and say 'It has great depth.' And there are times when we point to the same painting and say 'It is flat.' Alexander, having caught hold of these two, quite different, descriptions is troubled how to put them together. The painting cannot both have great depth and be flat— this sounds like a contradiction. Hence, he reasons, when we say the painting has depth we are suffering from an illusion.

I want to say that a Cezanne painting really does have great depth. We are not victimized by an illusion, nor are we suffering from an hallucination, when we say of the apples in a Cezanne still-life, that one apple is in front of the other. Nor are we speaking of what seems to be the case instead of what actually is the case. One apple is in front of the other, the painting does have great depth. Thus there is nothing to be explained away. But there is a confusion which must be eliminated. Let there be no mistake about what is being said here. Alexander says that the Madonna is flat, the "Hermes" is not divine but only seems so, the girls in the Spring are not in motion—they too only seem so. I cannot say whether the "Hermes" Alexander speaks of is divine or not, for I do not know which statue he is referring to. But if, when he speaks of the girls in the Spring, he is referring to Botticelli's "Primavera," then, of course, the girls are in motion. There is no question of it merely seeming to be the case, it is the case. Furthermore, let it be clear that it is the painting I am talking about, not some "illusory object" or "imaginary object" or a "series of intermittent perceptions."

There are many ways of describing a painting. We can say 'The painting is flat' and we can also say 'The painting has great depth.' We can say 'It is a painting of apples, all of which are about the same size, with some close up and others off in the distance.' We can also say 'It is a painting of apples, all of which are different sizes, some large and placed towards the bottom of the canvas, and others small at the top of the canvas.' (We can also describe what we see and speak of how the painting looks, but the use of this sort of description is not germane to our problem.) Difficulties arise only if we suppose that all of these descriptions have the same use, only if we confuse the use of these various descriptions.

We can imagine a curious sort of game that might be played here to clarify our problem. Suppose we set ourselves the task of describing a Cezanne painting, and we wished to describe it in all sorts of ways. First, we might say the painting is a flat pigment-coated strip of canvas mounted on wooden stretchers. If we were to go to a carpenter and ask him to build a crate for shipping the painting we might say to him 'The crate needn't be very wide; it will be used to ship an ordinary painting.' It would be important in this case for the carpenter to realize that the painting we wish to ship is made of a flat strip of canvas mounted on wooden stretchers, for some paintings are executed on gesso panels, some on masonite, and some on plaster slabs, and so forth. The width of the crate required might vary in different cases. Secondly, we might say the painting is a strip of linen canvas coated with pigments containing manganese oxides, iron hydroxides, and so forth. This would be important and relevant to a chemist engaged in cleaning the painting. It might also be of interest to someone planning to purchase the painting for he would probably wish to know whether the colors are especially apt to fade. Thirdly, we might say it is a painting of apples, all of which are different sizes, some large and placed toward the bottom of the canvas, and others small toward the top. This would be like describing a picture of two people, one close up and the other off in the distance, as a picture of one very big person and another very tiny person. Even this queer sort of description occasionally has a use. For example, it would be relevant to describe the picture as consisting of large and small apples to an art student intent on copying the painting; we might say to him 'You have drawn the apple towards the top of the canvas much too large. The one in the painting you are supposed to be copying is a very small apple.' Fourthly, we might say it is a painting of apples, all of which are about the same size, with some close up and others off in the distance. This is, perhaps, the most familiar kind of description of a painting. When we ask 'What is the painting of?' this is one sort of answer that might be relevant. In short, it is what we usually call a description of the subject-matter of the painting. Fifthly, we might say it is a painting with strong two-dimensional movements contrasted with a diagonal three-dimensional movement. Or we might say simply, the painting has great depth. This is the sort of description a person who criticizes, judges, evaluates, or simply appreciates the painting would be primarily interested in. There are of course still many other kinds of descriptions that might be given, but these are sufficient for our purposes.

Lest there be any misunderstanding of what has been said, let me say explicitly that in providing examples of how these various descriptions are sometimes used I do not wish to suggest that they are used only in the ways mentioned. This is plainly untrue. Nor do I wish to suggest that the examples given are to be taken as typical instances of how these various descriptions are used. Perhaps they are typical instances and perhaps they are not. I cannot say, for I am not at all sure how it could be shown either that they are typical instances or that they are not typical instances. And whether they are or are not typical instances is of no importance here. All I wish to suggest is that at least one kind of situation where we use such descriptions is the kind I have just mentioned. If this is granted then that is sufficient for the purposes of this discussion.

The first step in coping with the apparent "conflict" between the first and fifth descriptions is to realize that we have a similar "conflict" between the third and fourth descriptions. In one breath we can speak of two apples in the picture as being different sizes, one large and one small. In another breath we can also speak of the apples as being the same size, one in front of the other. We shall be in Alexander's dilemma if we feel that only one of these descriptions is the true description. If we feel inclined to say 'How can both of these accounts be true? Either the two apples pictured are the same size or they are not,' the same puzzle arises. What shall we say? Shall we say the two apples are the same size but they look different? Or shall we

15

say they are different sizes but they look alike? If we say they are the same size, in what way do they look different? Only in that one looks close up and the other looks off in the distance. When we say they are the same in size they also look the same size. If we say they are different in size, in what way do they look alike? When we say they are different sizes we can also say they look different sizes. All that we shall have done, in introducing descriptions of how the apples look, is to have introduced another pair of apparently "conflicting" descriptions. Now instead of the descriptions 'The apples are the same size' and 'The apples are different sizes' we have the descriptions 'The apples look the same size' and 'The apples look different sizes.' Thus we are not one jot better off than we were at the start. (And this is one way of seeing that the use of the descriptions of what we see and how things look is not germane to our problem.)

What we must realize here is that these apparently "conflicting" descriptions, the third with the fourth, the first with the fifth, do not in fact conflict with one another. They could conflict only if they were used in the same ways, in the same situation and for the same purposes. This is not the case, and that it is not must be quite clear. If we contrast the description 'The painting is flat'—when we use this description to inform a carpenter about the width of a crate required for shipping a painting, with the description 'The painting has great depth'—when we use this description to inform an art-critic about the structure of a painting, we can see that these two descriptions have nothing to do with one another. It would be absurd to tell the carpenter 'The painting has great depth' for he would suppose a wide crate was required. It would be equally absurd to tell the art-critic 'The painting is flat' for he would be astounded to hear that a Cezanne still-life had no depth. He might well reply 'Are you sure? Cezanne was a master in his treatment of space. Perhaps the painting is not an original?' If an art-critic tells us 'Many of Gauguin's paintings, unlike those of Cezanne, are flat' are we to say the critic is confused? Does he not know that all paintings are flat? If we told this to the critic he would probably reply in a justifiably irritable tone that he had no time to waste on this nonsense. If we did not learn enough about art when we were children to understand what he is talking about we had better go back to school and learn some more before we attempt to philosophize about art.

The description 'The painting is flat' which we use in speaking about a painting to an art-critic is radically unlike the description 'The painting is flat' which we use in speaking about a painting to a carpenter. If we do not take the notion too seriously it is useful here to speak of a family of descriptions; in this way we can speak of members of the carpenter's family of descriptions, and members of the art-critic's family, members of the chemist's family, and so forth. It is important to realize that often members of the carpenter's family look much like members of the art-critic's family. I have already pointed out that the descriptions 'The painting is flat' and 'The painting has depth' which belong to the critic's family have their doubles which belong to the carpenter's family. And note that the descriptions 'The painting looks flat' and 'The painting looks as if it has depth' which belong to the carpenter's family also have their doubles which belong to the critic's family. And there are many other sets of doubles; 'The painting is top-heavy,' 'The painting is fragile,' and so forth, all have their doubles. But we ordinarily have no trouble in telling them apart. The reason for this is that they rarely associate. Members of the carpenter's family hardly ever stray into an art gallery; if they do, they are apt to be thrown out by the critic who finds them dull company. The only time a member of the carpenter's family ever lingers in an art gallery is when he has been dragged in by the heels by some philosopher to be mated with a member of the critic's family.

Is it any wonder that such a union engenders a contradiction? But this is no excuse for the philosopher to claim that the members of the critic's family are all bastards. When we say 'The painting is flat' and then in another breath add 'but the painting has great depth' we are mixing up these two, quite different, descriptions in a horribly confused manner so as to yield a dilemma. There is in fact no conflict between these two descriptions; there is no need to try to explain away one in favor of the other.

Of course, in saying there is in fact no conflict between these two descriptions I do not wish to suggest that every time someone says 'The painting is flat but the painting has great depth' it is necessarily the case that in fact there is no conflict. This would be much like saying that it is necessarily the case that no one in fact could contradict himself. This certainly is not true. People are not in the habit of deliberately pronouncing explicit contradictions, but this is not to say that they could not do so if they chose. But the presumption is that if anyone does, in the ordinary run of things, say 'The painting is flat but it has great depth' he is not deliberately pronouncing an explicit contradiction, but rather, is mixing up two, quite different, descriptions, perhaps deliberately, so as to yield an apparent paradox. In such a case there is in fact no conflict between the two descriptions and, there is no need to attempt to explain away one in favor of the other. More significantly, there is no need, and it is a serious mistake, to suppose that there is some unique object corresponding to each different description. It is an error, and an error which has vitiated a good deal of recent aesthetics, to postulate some illusory or imaginary object to be the work of art. The ordinary painting hanging in the museum is the work of art, not some illusion or hallucination. There are not two things being referred to when we say, in the carpenter's shop, 'The painting is flat,' and when we say, in the gallery, 'The painting has great depth.' There is just one, and it is the painting. There are two descriptions, not two objects.

In concluding this essay I should like briefly to indicate one important point that I have not mentioned. And though I have not mentioned it, this point is important for there is good reason to believe that it is the source from which these other puzzles stem. To see just what this is, it is essential to notice that Alexander, along with other aestheticians, does not feel inclined to explain away the description 'The painting is flat' but he does wish to explain away the description 'The painting has great depth.' This is illuminating, for the fact that he does wish to explain away 'The painting has great depth' but does not wish to explain away 'The painting is flat' shows that he is troubled by the one description in a way that he is not by the other. Thus if we wish to get at the source of this difficulty, it is not sufficient to indicate, as I have done, that these two apparently conflicting descriptions do not in fact conflict and that they have radically different uses. What I must do is eliminate the difficulty aestheticians find in connection with our use of the description 'The painting has great depth.' This difficulty is, of course, how to settle disputes over whether or not a painting does have great depth, how to verify the statement 'The painting has great depth,' and so forth. Thus I am saying that aestheticians who try to explain away the description 'The painting has great depth' do so because they are inclined to believe that a dispute over the depth of a painting cannot be resolved. That is, they are inclined to say that in such a situation there is nothing that can be done to settle the issue, that we cannot establish either that the painting does have depth or that it does not have depth. Thus instead of saying 'The painting has great depth' they feel we should say, if we wish to speak properly, 'The painting seems to have great depth.' So the fundamental question is: Can we verify that the painting has great depth? And the answer is that, of course, we can. However, I do not propose to argue this point here.

The question has been mentioned only to indicate that it is a problem which must be dealt with before the ghost of aesthetics, the mysterious aesthetic object, can finally be laid to rest.

II

The Task of Defining
a Work of Art *

ONE of the foremost problems of aesthetics has been to provide a definition (or an analysis, or an explication, or an elucidation) of the notion of a work of art. The solutions given by aestheticians to this problem have often been violently opposed to one another; contrast Tolstoi's answer with that of his predecessors. There is no doubt that the problem is a difficult one. But what I should like to consider here is why it is so difficult. In this way I hope to make clear what is involved in such a definition and what an aesthetician must do, whether he knows it or not, to justify his definition of a work of art.

I

Suppose a child does not understand what a book is, is merely puzzled by people speaking about books. One of the many means at hand to help him grasp the use of that word 'book' would be simply to show him a book. But one would not help or try to help him by picking out a pocket book, or a diary with blank pages, or a loose-leaf notebook. What

* Revised from an essay originally published in *The Philosophical Review*, LXII (1953); reprinted by permission.

is wanted here is a perhaps fat book, but not too fat, with a hard cover, perhaps a gold-lettered leather-bound book. If someone does not know but wants to know what a table is, to learn the use of the word 'table,' it would not do to begin by showing him an esoteric table with ninety-six legs, only six inches high. Again one would take a good solid oak table with a modest number of legs, an ordinary, everyday sort of table, not a cabinet maker's nightmare. If we begin with a clear-cut case, one no one would ordinarily be tempted to dispute, we can then shift to the less clear-cut, the disputed, cases. A clear-cut case is a place to start from.

What would a clear-cut case of a work of art be? One is inclined to say a painting like Poussin's "The Rape of the Sabine Women," or Da Vinci's "Mona Lisa," or Rembrandt's "Night Watch," would do here, that no one would want to object. But suppose one were to say, 'No, none of these are works of art.' If, when we pointed to an ordinary everyday sort of table, one were to object, 'No, that's not a table,' we could and should say he was clearly confused, in one way or another. Maybe he imagined we had not pointed at the table, that we had pointed at a chair; or we might suppose that he supposed the word 'table' was only and always applied to multiplication tables; and so forth. Perhaps cultivated confusion at a sophisticated level, but nothing else but confusion, could be the root of a dispute over our clear-cut example of a table; but a refusal to call the Poussin, or the Da Vinci, or even the Rembrandt a work of art, need not be the blossom of a merely blooming confusion. It is in fact possible to dispute whether any particular painting is a work of art or not, and people do dispute such questions, in a way that it is not in fact possible to dispute whether any particular object is a table or not.

And this is to say simply that there are and can be no clear-cut cases of works of art in quite the same sense as there can be such clear-cut cases of tables or chairs. That this is so stems partly from the fact that there are many uses of the phrase 'work of art' in a way in which there are very few uses of the word 'table.' (Even though the word 'table' does have many diverse uses, one can speak of multiplication tables, dinner tables, table lands, there are very few uses of the word 'table' in connection with those ordinary everyday objects that one customarily sits at and eats off, tables. But in this sense, there are many distinct and different and even "competing" uses of the phrase 'work of art.') It also stems partly from the fact that among these many uses of the phrase 'work of art,' some are aptly described as laudatory or eulogistic. The many reasons why this is so will, I trust, become clear in the course of this discussion. For the time being, even though the examples of works of art which I have cited might not or need not be accepted by everyone, they are the clearest cases available, and as such they provide a useful base for our explorations.

In selecting a clear-cut example of a carpenter's hammer, one could choose a hammer with a handle exactly twelve and three-quarters inches long. Perhaps the title of the book we pointed to, the leather-bound book with gold lettering, was *Anna Karenina*. But in describing or talking about the example of a hammer to a child who did not grasp the use of the word, one would not say, 'The handle of the hammer is exactly twelve and three-quarters inches long.' Instead, one would be much more apt to say, 'The handle of the hammer is about a foot long,' or something of that sort. In the kind of case I have envisaged, the former statement would, at best, be misleading. Whether a description is liable to mislead depends roughly on why it is wanted. In describing the clear-cut case of a hammer, when we want to help someone understand how the word 'hammer' is used, we mention those facts about the object that make it, in fact, such a clear-cut case. That is why we would not say, 'The handle of the hammer is exactly twelve and three-quarters inches long.' This really does not matter; it does not affect and is entirely irrelevant to the status of the example as a clear-cut case. But the fact that the handle is about a foot long is really relevant here. Similarily, we would not mention the particular title of the book, which we were using as a clear-cut case; but the fact that it had a title would be relevant.

Suppose we point to Poussin's "The Rape of the Sabine Women" as our clearest available case of a work of art. We could describe it by saying, first, that it is a painting. Secondly, it was made, and what is more, made deliberately and self-consciously with obvious skill and care, by Nicolas Poussin. Thirdly, the painter intended it to be displayed in a place where it could be looked at and appreciated, where it could be contemplated and admired. In short, he intended it to be treated in a way much like the way that works of art are customarily treated. In saying this I do not wish to suggest that Poussin intended his work to be exhibited in a museum gallery. I do not know, but I would suppose the painting was intended to be hung in some chateau, or something of the sort. So perhaps in this respect the painting is not treated in the way intended by the painter. But there is good reason to believe that the painter did intend the painting to be displayed in an appropriate manner, to be treated with care, and to be preserved for as long as possible. And there is good reason to believe that Poussin did intend the painting to be contemplated, studied, observed, admired, criticized, and discussed by some people, if not by just any people. Fourthly, the painting is or was exhibited in a museum gallery where people do contemplate, study, observe, admire, criticize, and discuss it. What I wish to refer to here by speaking of contemplating, studying, and observing a painting, is simply what we may do when we are concerned with a painting like this. For example, when we look at this painting by Poussin, we may attend to its sensuous features, to its "look and feel." Thus we attend to the play of light and color, to dissonances, contrasts, and harmonies of hues, values, and intensities. We notice patterns and pigmentation, textures, decorations, and embellishments. We may also attend to the structure, design, composition, and organization of the work. Thus we look for unity, and we also look for variety, for balance and movement. We attend to the formal interrelations and cross connections in the work, to its underlying structure. We are concerned with both two-dimensional and three-dimensional movements, the balance and opposition, thrust and recoil, of spaces and volumes. We attend to the sequences, overlaps, and rhythms of line, form, and color. We may also attend to the expressive, significant, and symbolic aspects of the work. Thus we attend to the subject matter, to the scene depicted, and to the interrelations between the formal structure and the scene portrayed. We attend to the emotional character of the presented forms, and so forth. This is, roughly, what I have in mind when I speak of contemplating, studying, and observing this Poussin painting. (Lest there be any misunderstanding, let me say explicitly that I am not saying that when ordinary people either contemplate or study or observe or attend to or look at or in any way concern themselves with this Poussin painting, they do in fact always attend to or concern themselves with all of the aspects of the painting that I have here mentioned. This is plainly untrue. But it is true that some people, when they look at this painting, are concerned with some of its many aspects that I have mentioned, while other people concern themselves with other of its aspects. And it is true, certainly, that all of these aspects of the painting are attended to at one time or another, and occasionally even all by one very unordinary person at one time.) Fifthly, this work is a representational painting with a definite subject matter; it depicts a certain mythological scene. Sixthly, the painting has an elaborate and certainly complex formal structure. Finally, the painting is a good painting. And this is to say simply that the Poussin painting is worth contemplating, studying, and observing in the way I have ever so roughly described.

It must be clear that whether the Poussin painting does or does not in fact fit the description that I have given is irrelevant to what I am saying. For example, it is at least within the nebulous realm of possibility that I am much mistaken in saying it is a good painting. It is even more than merely possible that I have been misinformed about Poussin's intentions. Maybe I have made other mistakes as well. But whether this is so or not does not in the least matter, for I am not trying to show that the Poussin painting is in fact a work of art. Rather I am trying to clarify what may be meant by saying that the Poussin painting is a work of art. What is important here is this: Because I believe the Poussin painting does fit the description I have given, I believe that it is, and I have chosen it as, one of the clearest available cases of a work of art. Our concern here is only with the description and not with whether the description fits the particular case. Each of the various facts mentioned in the foregoing description are characteristic of a work of art, it is these characteristics that concern us.

In order to make clear what the difficulties are in formulating and justifying a definition of a work of art, in the following section I shall present what I take to be an adequate definition based on the preceding account of the Poussin painting. However, I shall not here attempt to show that the definition is in fact adequate.

II

All of the characteristics mentioned in the preceding description of the Poussin painting together constitute a set of characteristics. Several characteristics taken together constitute a set of characteristics if and only if all of the characteristics mentioned are relevant in determining whether something is or is not a work of art and if they are

the only characteristics that are so relevant. Anything pos-
sessing all of these characteristics can then be said to be a
characteristic case. Consequently, if the Poussin painting
does in fact fit the description given above, it is such a
characteristic case.

The set of characteristics given provides us with a set of
sufficient conditions for something's being a work of art.
Anything clearly satisfying these conditions can be said to
be a work of art in exactly the same sense of the phrase
'work of art' in which the Poussin painting can be said to
be a work of art. It is important to notice that I said "clearly
satisfying these conditions." The word 'clearly' is crucial
here. There is a temptation to say that the preceding description of the Poussin painting provides nothing more
than a rough schema of what could be said about the work.
This is not quite true, but it is a way of emphasizing the
truth that there is a great deal of latitude in the various
details of the description given. For example, one of the
facts mentioned about the Poussin painting was that it is
a representational work. Suppose we now consider a statue
by Praxiteles: are we to say that it is representational? Someone might say that a statue cannot be representational in
quite the same sense in which a painting can be. On the
other hand, it could be claimed that both a statue and a
painting can be said to be representational, in the very
same sense of the word, but that they are merely different
species of representative works. Again, someone might say
that a sculptor does not make a statue in quite the same
sense in which a painter makes his painting. And again it
could be said that there is no difference in sense but only a
difference in species. And this kind of question can be raised
in connection with each of the characteristics mentioned.

I take it that we are inclined to speak of a difference in
sense when we are impressed by, or wish to stress, dissimilarities. But when we are impressed by, or wish to stress,
similarities, we are then inclined to speak of a mere dif-

ference in species. By speaking of a case that "clearly" satisfies the conditions given above, I mean to refer to a case in which there is no inclination to speak of a shift in sense with respect to any of the characteristics listed. Unless this point is attended to, it might mistakenly seem that we do not have a set of sufficient conditions, for one can conjure up some curious cases.

Suppose an object were found, satisfying the conditions given above, but with this one eccentricity: the scene depicted, and consequently the formal structure as well, changed periodically, without being changed. Imagine an object fitting the description, but having the peculiarity that, without being moved, it moved occasionally about the room. Thus in a way these odd objects behave somewhat like living organisms. One could be reluctant to call these things works of art. It could be difficult to know what to say. Shall we say that our set of characteristics does not, therefore, provide a set of sufficient conditions? We have not mentioned the fact that the object is a stable object, that it does not change or move about periodically of its own accord. This would be a mistake. We should be uncertain whether these odd objects were works of art solely because we should be uncertain whether they did in fact fit the description which we have given. It would be queer to say of an object that it was a painting and that it periodically moved about the room of its own accord. It would be equally queer to say of an object that it was a painting depicting a certain scene and that the scene periodically changed of its own accord. Facts like these cast doubt on whether the object is a painting in the sense of the word 'painting' originally intended, and on whether the painting depicts a scene in the sense of the phrase 'depicts a scene' originally intended. But if an object does clearly satisfy the conditions stated, there can be no doubt but that it can be said to be a work of art in the very same sense of the phrase 'work of art' in which the Poussin painting can be said to be a work of art.

Although the above set of characteristics provides a set of sufficient conditions, it does not provide a set of necessary and sufficient conditions. No one of the characteristics listed is necessarily a characteristic of a work of art. But a definition in terms of necessary and sufficient conditions is merely one kind of definition, one way of describing the use of a word or phrase. Another kind of definition, and the kind we are here concerned with, is one in terms of various subsets of a set of characteristics, or, in less exotic language, in terms of similarities to what I have called a characteristic case, a case in which an entire set of characteristics is exemplified.[1] The following examples should serve to clarify what is meant by speaking of similarities to a characteristic case.

Suppose we have a naturally formed stone object that has the shape of a woman reclining. Indeed, it looks as though some sculptor has fashioned it, though we know that this is not the case. What is more, it is worth contemplating, studying, and observing in a way analogous to the way described in connection with the Poussin painting. Further suppose that people do in fact contemplate, study, and observe it, that it is displayed in a museum, and so forth. In virtue of its similarities to the characteristic case, this object can be said to be a work of art. The points of similarity between this object and the Poussin painting constitute a particular subset of the set of characteristics listed above. Imagine this sort of case: We have a nonrepresentational

[1] I am deeply indebted to Max Black, both through his published papers and from discussions with him, for many of the ideas in this paper. In particular, I have, I trust, here profited from his account of a definition in terms of overlapping and interacting criteria. See Max Black, "The Definition of Scientific Method," *Science and Civilization*, ed. R. C. Stauffer.

painting, deliberately made by an artist, who intended it to be exhibited and displayed, and who wanted people to contemplate, study, and observe it. But in fact the painting is not worth contemplating, studying, and observing. What is more, no one does bother with it at all. It is not exhibited, displayed, and so forth; rather it is buried away in some cellar. This too, in virtue of its similarities to the characteristic case, can be said to be a work of art. Again, the points of similarity between this work and the characteristic case constitute another subset of the set of characteristics given above.

In each of the preceding examples, when it was said that the object was a work of art in virtue of its similarities to the characteristic case, it was implicitly assumed that the similarities noted were sufficient to warrant the claim that the objects were works of art. No rule can be given to determine what is or is not a sufficient degree of similarity to warrant such a claim. If for one reason or another the dissimilarities become impressive (and what impresses one need not impress another), one is then reluctant to call the object a work of art. For example, a Greek vase is, in many ways, similar to a New England bean pot. Both are artifacts; both were made to serve domestic purposes; neither was intended to stand in a museum; and so forth. Nonetheless, a Greek vase is a work of art while a New England bean pot is not. To see that this is so, consider those points of similarity between a Greek vase and the Poussin painting that are also points of dissimilarity between a Greek vase and a New England bean pot. We do not, in fact, treat a New England bean pot in a way similar to the way we treat the Poussin painting; whereas we do, in fact, treat a Greek vase in a way quite similar to the way we treat the Poussin painting. We set up Greek vases on pedestals; we do display and exhibit them in museums and galleries, and what is more, it is worth while to do so. We do not in fact contemplate, study, observe, admire, criticize, and discuss bean pots in a way that we do Greek vases or in the way that we do the Poussin painting; furthermore, it seems most unlikely that it would be worth while to do so. Unlike bean pots, and like the Poussin painting, many Greek vases are representational. One is inclined to speak, and one does speak, of the formal structure of a Greek vase in a way similar to the way one speaks of the formal structure of the Poussin painting. We do not, in fact, speak of the formal structure of a bean pot, nor is there usually any inclination to do so. If one starts, as it were, from the Poussin painting and then shifts to the Greek vase, one begins to feel the strain. A Greek vase was not (or so we are supposing) intended to be treated in a way similar to the way the Poussin painting is treated. It was designed to fulfill a specific utilitarian function. Many Greek vases are not representational. They were not, in the time of the Greeks (or so we are supposing), set up on pedestals. They were not displayed and exhibited in museums and galleries. They were not contemplated, studied, observed, admired, criticized, and discussed in a way similar to the way in which the Poussin painting is. One begins to feel the strain in speaking of a Greek vase as a work of art. Now if one tries to speak of a bean pot as a work of art, the strain becomes too great. We have reached a breaking point, and one is inclined to say things like, 'A bean pot *cannot* be classed as a work of art.' It is only a matter of degree.

Finally, neither a poem, nor a novel, nor a musical composition can be said to be a work of art in the same sense of the phrase in which a painting or a statue or a vase can be said to be a work of art. Such things as poems, novels, musical compositions, possess none of the characteristics listed in our set of characteristics; a poem is not exhibited or displayed; one does not contemplate, study, and observe a poem; a poem is not representational; and so forth. And even though a poem may seem to possess some of the characteristics listed, for one can and does speak of a good poem,

31

the dissimilarities between what is meant in speaking of a good poem and what is meant in speaking of a good painting are sufficiently impressive to warrant our saying it is a different sense of the word 'good.' All of this, however, does not show that one cannot reasonably use the phrase 'work of art' to refer to poems, novels, musical compositions, as well as to paintings. If one wished to describe a use of the phrase 'work of art' in which there is such a systematic shift in sense, one could do so in terms of several sets of characteristics. One would take a clear-cut case of a poem and obtain a set of characteristics, then a clear-cut case of a novel and obtain another set, and so forth. Then something would be a work of art, in this use of the phrase, if it possessed some subset of the set of characteristics pertaining to paintings, or some subset of the set of characteristics pertaining to poems, and so forth. This may seem an extremely complex way of using the phrase 'work of art,' but it is actually often used in somewhat this way by critics who speak of the 'art of painting,' the 'art of poetry,' and so forth. Such a "blanket" use of the phrase may be warranted by the fact, if it is a fact, that each set of characteristics is analogous in composition to every other set; the analogue of contemplating a painting is reading a poem, the analogue of a good painting is a good poem, the analogue of display is publish, and so forth.

There is no need to elaborate this definition any further for the purposes of this discussion. The preceding account is sufficiently explicit to stir up and bring to the surface all the important difficulties that must be noted here.

III

The definition just given provides a rough description of only one use of the phrase 'work of art.' But this phrase is and has been used in many ways. So long as art remains what it has always been, something changing and varied, so long as there are artistic revolutions, the phrase 'work of art,' or some equivalent locution, will continue to be used in many ways. For when such revolutions occur, there is inevitably a shift in some uses of the phrase 'work of art.' Some understanding of the nature of the disputes that occur over what is and what is not a work of art during such periods of artistic revolution is essential to an understanding of what an aesthetician is doing in offering some one, and only one, definition of a work of art.

When nonrepresentational and abstract painting first attracted attention in the early part of this century, many people complained bitterly that the nonrepresentational and abstract works were not works of art. Thus one critic wrote: "The farce will end when people look at Post-Impressionist pictures as Mr. Sargent looked at those shown in London, 'absolutely skeptical as to their having any claim whatever to being works of art.' " [2] Other critics insisted, with equal vehemence, that the Post-Impressionist paintings most certainly were works of art. If one looks with an impartial eye at these disputes between the traditional and the modern critics, one thing is clear. In many cases the parties to the disputes were using the phrase 'work of art' in more or less different ways. Indeed, the modern critics, the defenders of the new works, were introducing a more or less novel use of the phrase. To see that this is so, it is necessary to attend to some of the typical complaints that were voiced against modern art by the traditional critics.

In a review of the first exhibition of modern art in America, Mr. Kenyon Cox claimed that

the real meaning of this Cubist movement is nothing else than the total destruction of the art of painting—that art of which the dictionary definition is "the art of representing, by means of figures and colors applied on a surface, objects presented to the eye or to the imagination." . . . Now the total destruction of painting as a representative art is a thing which a lover of

[2] Royal Cortissoz, "The Post-Impressionist Illusion," *Three Papers on "Modernist Art,"* p. 42.

painting could hardly envisage with entire equanimity, yet one may admit that such a thing might take place and yet an art remain that should have its own value. A Turkish rug or a tile from the Alhambra is nearly without representative purpose, but it has intrinsic beauty and some conceivable use. The important question is what it is proposed to substitute for this art of painting which the world has cherished since there were men definitely differentiated from beasts. Having abolished the representation of nature and all forms of recognized and traditional decoration, what will the "modernists" give us instead? [3]

It is often erroneously supposed that traditional critics held representation to be a necessary characteristic of a work of art. This is not true. Such critics did maintain that it was a relevant characteristic, but few insisted it was necessary in that without representation there could be no work of art. What is true is that traditional critics weighted this characteristic enormously, so that it was of paramount importance in determining whether a given work was or was not a work of art. In their reaction against this view, some of the modern critics have apparently gone to the extreme of suggesting that representation is wholly irrelevant to art.[4] In this respect, our definition would be apt to satisfy neither a conservative traditional critic nor an extreme modern critic. The shift in the notion of a work of art that was brought about through the modern developments was, with respect to the question of representation, primarily a shift in emphasis, and only secondarily a shift with respect to necessary conditions. The point is that representation was of paramount importance in virtue of the fact that "accurate" representation played the role of a necessary condition in determining what was and was not a good painting. This leads us to another point of difference between the traditional and modern critics.

[3] "The 'Modern' Spirit in Art," *ibid.*, pp. 6–8.
[4] See Clive Bell, *Art*, pp. 28–30, where such a view is, or seems to be, suggested.

34

I am inclined to suppose both traditional and modern critics would accept the seventh characteristic listed in our definition, viz., that the work be a good one, as a relevant characteristic of a work of art. (Whether they considered it to be a necessary characteristic is a difficult question that need not concern us here.) But it is fairly obvious that what the traditional critics meant in speaking of a good painting or a good drawing was somewhat different from what the modern critics meant. For example, Mr. Royal Cortissoz, in reviewing the first exhibition of modern art in America, severely criticized Van Gogh's drawing.

The laws of perspective are strained. Landscape and other natural forms are set awry. So simple an object as a jug containing some flowers is drawn with the uncouthness of the immature, even childish, executant. From the point of view of the Post-Impressionist prophet, all this may be referred to inventive genius beating out a new artistic language. I submit that it is explained rather by incompetence suffused with egotism.[5]

Somewhat later in his review, while discussing Matisse's drawing, Mr. Cortissoz stated that

whatever his ability may be, it is swamped in the contortions of his misshapen figures. The fact is that real genius in these matters will out. Degas, who has been all his life a disciple of Ingres, uses a magic of draftmanship akin to that of his idol, though the style and spirit of his work are wholly his own.[6]

It is, I take it, fairly clear that Mr. Cortissoz' notion of a good drawing, of a good painting, would today be objected to. For he, together with most traditional critics, apparently held that a necessary condition (though not, of course, a sufficient condition as is sometimes naïvely supposed) for a drawing to be considered a good drawing is that the perspective be "true," the form "realistic," and so forth. Few if any critics today would subscribe to this view.

Perhaps the clearest indication of the fact that the mod-

[5] *Op. cit.*, p. 31.   [6] *Ibid.*, pp. 36–37.

ern critics were using the phrase 'work of art' in a more or less novel way is to be found in the oft-repeated charge that the new works had broken with tradition. In claiming that there had been such a break, the traditional critics can be taken as claiming that the degree of similarity between the new works and those accepted in the tradition as works of art was insufficient to warrant the claim that the new works were works of art. The dissimilarities were felt to be overwhelming; the gap was held to be too great to bridge. The modern critics, of course, denied that there had been any such rupture, at least not with the tradition as they saw it; rather they insisted that tradition had been reasonably extended and developed. They repudiated the charge of a complete break by exhuming and pointing to the works of such people as El Greco to justify the modern use of distortion, just as somewhat later the Surrealists were to exhume the works of Acrimboldo and Bosch in an effort to make their own fantasies more palatable to the public. It is for this reason, among others, that the works of Matisse have so often been compared with Egyptian portraits, Japanese prints, and so forth, while the similarities between Picasso's work and practically everything in any tradition have been set forth exhaustively. Whether modern art did in fact break with European tradition is not a point that need concern us. But the fact that the tradition was at least extended cannot be denied and is here relevant. For this is merely another way of saying that there was some shift in the notion of a work of art. Let it be quite clear that I am not claiming to have here shown that the modern critics were introducing a somewhat novel use of the phrase 'work of art.' To show that such was the case, it would be necessary to present a great deal more evidence than I have done. But everything about the disputes between the traditional and the modern critics certainly suggests that the modern critics were in fact using the phrase 'work of art' in a somewhat novel way. If the likelihood of this is granted, that is sufficient for the purposes of this discussion.

Once it is realized that the modern critics were most likely using the phrase 'work of art' in a somewhat novel way, there is, or is apt to be, a temptation to say that the disputes between the traditional and the modern critics were merely verbal. One may be inclined to say that in a modern critic's use of the phrase, the new works were in fact works of art, while in a traditional critic's use, they were not. This is a temptation which we must certainly resist. Even though it may be true that the new works were works of art in a modern critic's use of the phrase, and were not works of art in a traditional critic's use, it would be absurd to think that, therefore, the disputes were merely verbal. The disputes, in part, arose from conflicting decisions over the way to use the phrase 'work of art,' but such decisions were not and certainly need not be thought arbitrary. Decisions may not be true or false, but they can be reasonable or unreasonable, wise or unwise. In effect, the traditional critics maintained that their decision to use the phrase 'work of art' in a traditional way was the most reasonable one, and consequently their use of the phrase was the most reasonable use; the modern critics made exactly the same claim in favor of their own somewhat radical use of the phrase. Sometimes these claims were made explicitly; at other times, such a claim is implicit in the criticism, favorable or unfavorable, given to the new works. To understand what is involved in such a claim and what is meant by speaking of a "reasonable use" of a word or phrase, it is necessary to see why it may be important to use a word or phrase in one way rather than another, and what there is that may be worth arguing about.

IV

There is no sense in speaking of a "reasonable use" of a word or phrase *in vacuo*. What is or is not a reasonable use depends on the particular context in which the question is raised, on the kind of considerations involved, and so forth. For example, if you want to be understood, you are well advised to use your words in some ordinary and familiar way; but if being understood is not at issue, this advice is not to the point. Not being understood may be one consequence of using a word or phrase in a particular way, but there may be other consequences, and consequences of a different kind. For example, it is, I suppose, no part of the meaning or the use of the phrase 'excessive speed' that if a driver of a vehicle involved in an accident is held to have been driving at an excessive speed, he is likely to suffer certain penalties under the law. But even though this may be said to be no part of the use of the phrase, it is nevertheless an important fact which a jurist must keep in mind when attempting to specify the use of the phrase in a court of law. It would be unwise, for example, to lay down a ruling that would constitute a precedent for taking excessive speed to be any speed over posted limits. A man may drive at a speed greater than the posted limit in an attempt to avoid an impending accident. It would be unreasonable to penalize him for making the attempt if it happened that even so he was unable to avoid the accident.

What I am saying is that once the legal consequences and implications of declaring a person to have been driving at an excessive speed are relatively fixed, we can then, in the light of these consequences and on the basis of certain moral and legal notions concerning the purposes to be accomplished by means of these consequences, say what is or is not a reasonable definition and a reasonable use of the phrase 'excessive speed' in a court of law. (One can, of course, reverse this process and argue that once the notion of excessive speed is fairly well fixed in the sense indicated above, it is unreasonable to penalize a man merely for driving at an excessive speed. Thus someone could argue that his use of the phrase in the sense indicated above was reasonable, the consequences that are likely to occur in the course of using the phrase unreasonable. In a sense, the use of the phrase and the significant legal consequences likely to occur in the course of using the phrase each provide a standpoint for criticism. We can criticize either the use of the phrase in terms of the fairly fixed legal consequences or the legal consequences in terms of the fairly fixed use.)

To ask 'What are the consequences and implications of something's being considered a work of art?' is to ask an equivocal question to which there can be no univocal answer. We must know in what context we are to suppose the phrase 'work of art' is being used. (Just so one can speak of the consequences of using the phrase 'excessive speed' in one way or another only when the context is specified. In a court of law the use of such a phrase may have significant consequences which, in some other context, simply are not forthcoming.) In the context where critical disputes are carried on, there are in fact many significant consequences arising from the fact that a certain type of work is considered a work of art. Disputes between critics are not private affairs. They are carried on in a social context, and they are significant only when set in the framework provided by such a context.

It is, I suppose, no part of the meaning or the use of the phrase 'work of art' that if a certain type of work is considered a work of art, works of this type will eventually find their way into a public museum. Nonetheless, public funds will, in fact, be spent on these works. The public will be advised to see and study such works. Books will be written and read about them, and so on. These are in fact some of the present characteristic social consequences of something's being considered a work of art in Western society. The social consequences and implications of something's being considered a work of art have varied in time, and no doubt they will continue to do so. They are merely an aspect of the particular role art plays in a particular society, and as the character of the society changes, the role of art in the society may also change, together with the characteristic social consequences and implications of something's being considered a work of art in that society. Although the traditional and the modern critics almost certainly disagreed about the specific characteristics of a work of art, they agreed both in their desires and in their expectations with regard to the characteristic social consequences and implications of something's being considered a work of art. Their agreement in this respect lent substance to their disputes over the use of the phrase 'work of art.' Indeed, the traditional critics explicitly and with great vehemence maintained that the Post-Impressionist works ought not to be placed in museums; that the public funds ought not to be spent on them; that the public would be ill-advised to spend its time looking at them or reading books about them; and so forth. All of this the modern critics explicitly and emphatically denied. (And this is one obvious reason why it would be quite absurd to call such disputes merely verbal.) To determine whether a certain type of work ought or ought not to be placed in a museum, purchased with public funds, and so on, it is necessary to consider what purposes it is to serve when once it has been purchased, when public funds have been spent on it, and so on. This is to say that in order to determine what is or is not a reasonable use of the phrase 'work of art,' it is necessary to consider not only the characteristic social consequences and implications of something's being considered a work of art, but also the purposes to be accomplished by means of these consequences—the various functions of a work of art in society. The role that the functions of a work of art play in determining whether a particular use of the phrase 'work of art' is reasonable or not, may be clarified by the following example.

Consider the second characteristic mentioned in our definition of a work of art, that the work be made, deliberately and self-consciously with obvious skill and care, by some person. The traditional view would be that this is a necessary characteristic of a work of art. In *Art as Experience*, John Dewey writes:

Suppose, for the sake of illustration, that a finely wrought object, one whose texture and proportions are highly pleasing in perception, has been believed to be a product of some primitive people. Then there is discovered evidence that proves it to be an accidental natural product. As an external thing, it is now precisely what it was before. Yet at once it ceases to be a work of art and becomes a natural "curiosity." It now belongs in a museum of natural history, not in a museum of art.[7]

I am much inclined to object to Dewey's use of the phrase 'work of art,' but it is unlikely that such an objection can be made directly on the grounds that his use of the phrase is unreasonable. To see why this is so, it is necessary to see precisely what is at issue here. This may appear to be a relatively trivial point, one hardly worth disputing over; there may in fact be fairly few natural objects that one is inclined to exhibit and display. What is and what is not excluded from a museum is in this case, however, of only secondary importance. The exclusion of a natural object from a museum of art is primarily of interest when viewed as symptomatic of a particular orientation toward the works that are in fact displayed in a museum. If one adopts a view similar to that of Dewey, there is a tendency to treat the work of art primarily as a "manifestation" of the artistic activity engaged in by the person who produced the object. One is then tempted to look through the work of art to the artist's "experiences," "feelings," and so forth. Furthermore, one is tempted to say that this "revealing" aspect of the work is essential to its functions as a work of art. The relevance of the artist's "experiences" to an appreciation of his work is an extremely complex problem which I shall not even attempt to consider here. But I mention these points

[7] Page 48.

in order to stress the fact that such considerations as these are relevant in attempting to determine whether the fact that the object was made by a person is or is not a necessary condition for its being a work of art. To claim that Dewey's traditional use of the phrase 'work of art' is unreasonable would, in effect, be to claim that the mere fact that an object is an artifact does not suffice to show that it is thereby incapable of satisfactorily fulfilling the various functions of a work of art. But since such a claim would be made on the basis of a particular view of these functions, Dewey's use of the phrase ought properly to be considered in relation to his own view of what these functions are or ought to be.

There is no doubt but that the explicit disagreements between the traditional and the modern critics stemmed from more or less divergent conceptions of what the functions of a work of art are or ought to be in our society. In writing of the first exhibition of Post-Impressionist works in England, Roger Fry pointed out that the new movement in art "implied a reconsideration of the very purpose and aim as well as methods of pictorial and plastic art." [8] He characterized the purpose of the new art by saying it was devoted to "the direct expression of feeling" and to the making of "images which by the clearness of their logical structure, and by their closely knit unity of texture, shall appeal to our disinterested and contemplative imagination with something of the same vividness as the things of actual life appeal to our practical activities." [9]

What Mr. Fry says here is, of course, quite vague, but he was dealing with an extraordinarily difficult topic. Vague or not, he is quite right in suggesting that modern works serve somewhat different purposes from the accepted works that had preceded them, no matter how difficult it may be to say precisely wherein the difference lies. To consider but one aspect of this enormously complicated question, a traditional view of a function of a work of art was that it was

[8] *Vision and Design*, p. 194.   [9] *Ibid.*, p. 195.

to constitute an object of Beauty, which would inspire, profit, and delight the beholder. 'Beauty' is not a term likely to be applied to a host of modern works, e.g., to one like Picasso's "Guernica." "Guernica" is no doubt a magnificent, powerful, superbly conceived and executed work, but it is not a thing of "Beauty." It is true that there are many paintings in European tradition to which one would be equally reluctant to apply the term 'Beauty,' Grünewald's "Crucifixion" in the Isenheim altarpiece, but it is also true that the obvious religious purpose of the Isenheim altarpiece is something more or less alien to modern art. That modern works do in fact serve somewhat different purposes from the accepted works that had preceded them is perhaps best signalized by the technical innovations introduced and employed by the modern artists. The extent of these innovations must not be underestimated.

It is true that the modern use of distortion has its analogue in El Greco's work among others, but it is also true that El Greco's work was practically ignored until the twentieth century. And of course even his work appears naturalistic in contrast with a work like "Les Demoiselles d'Avignon." To feel the full impact of the modern innovations in the use of color, it is merely necessary to see a work by Miro hung in a gallery alongside works done before 1850. Again one may admit that Poussin employed intense hues, and Giotto's work must have been quite brilliant at one time; but it is impossible to ignore the fact that many modern painters such as Miro and Matisse employ huge flat masses of color in an altogether new way, a way that is simply incompatible with and wholly alien to the spatial character of a Poussin painting. These and many other such technical innovations all herald the fact that modern paintings are devoted to somewhat different purposes and aims from those of the works that had preceded them. For the widespread adoption of new methods of working in art has, in fact, always been correlative to a more or less radical variation in the purposes and aims of art. (Just so the technical innovations of the monodic revolution in music at the beginning of the seventeenth century, the development of the so-called *stile moderno* or *seconda prattica* with its use of the thorough bass, the introduction of the recitative, and so forth, were the technical correlates of the development of secular music. Indeed, in the eyes of the modern critics of the period, the *stile antico* was seen as the sacred style appropriate to church music.)

Whether the traditional critics' disapproval of the purposes and aims of the new works stemmed from a failure to understand fully what these purposes and aims were, or whether this disapproval was based on a full understanding, is a purely historical question that need not concern us here. That they did disapprove is beyond question, for they voiced this disapproval in no uncertain terms; in concluding his review of the first exhibition of modern art in America, Mr. Cox adjured his readers to remember that

it is for you that art is created, and judge honestly for yourselves whether this which calls itself art is useful to you or to the world. You are not infallible, but, in the main, your instincts are right, and, after all, you are the final judges. If your stomach revolts against this rubbish it is because it is not fit for human food.[10]

Most aestheticians today, I believe, would say the modern critics were right in contending that the Post-Impressionist paintings were works of art. Indeed, few people now dare to question the status of modern art as art, and those who do are at once labeled "Philistines" and "reactionaries." But if we say the modern critics were right—and I do not presume to question the matter here—if we say their decision to use the phrase 'work of art' in a somewhat new way was a wise one and their use of the phrase was the most reasonable, we must not rashly assume that the traditional

[10] *Op. cit.*, p. 18.

critics' use of the phrase 'work of art' could be held to be unreasonable when examined on the basis of the traditional critics' own view of what the functions, purposes, and aims of a work of art are or ought to be. On the contrary, it is most likely that when so considered, their use of the phrase would prove to be quite reasonable. Thus an objection to their use of the phrase would most likely have to be made, and no doubt could be made, in terms of a prior objection to their view of what the functions of a work of art are or ought to be. (For one can reasonably dispute over the question of what the functions of a work of art are or ought to be just as one can reasonably dispute over what is or is not a reasonable use of the phrase 'work of art.') In accepting the modern critics' decision, we are, in effect, accepting something of their view of what the present functions, purposes, and aims of a work of art are or ought to be in our society.

What then is an aesthetician doing when he offers some one and only one definition of a work of art? It should be clear that he is not describing the actual use of the phrase. As I have tried to indicate above, this phrase is and has been used in many ways. No one definition can mirror this manifold and varying usage. Instead, an aesthetician is describing one, perhaps new, use of the phrase 'work of art,' which he either implicitly or explicitly claims to be the most reasonable use of the phrase in the light of the characteristic social consequences and implications of something's being considered a work of art, and on the basis of what the functions, purposes, and aims of a work of art are or ought to be in our society. What these purposes and aims are or ought to be is a matter of here and now. As the character of society changes, as new methods of working are developed, these purposes and aims will also change. With the development of new means there will be new ends that can be served, and with the appearance of new ends, new means will have to be developed to serve them. Art neither repeats itself nor stands still; it cannot if it is to remain art. An attempt to provide a definition and a justification of a definition of a work of art is, as R. G. Collingwood has stated, not "an attempt to investigate and expound eternal verities concerning the nature of an eternal object called Art"; rather it is an attempt to provide "the solution of certain problems arising out of the situation in which artists find themselves here and now." [11] An aesthetician is not and certainly ought not to be expected to be a seer foreseeing the future of art. He is not an oracle, though he may choose to speak like one. As new and different kinds of works are created, as the character of society changes and the role of art in society varies, as it has so often done throughout history, it may and most likely will be necessary to revise our definition of a work of art.

[11] *The Principles of Art*, p. vi.

III

Reasons in Art Criticism *

HSIEH HO said one of the principles of painting is that "through organization, place and position should be determined." Le Brun praised Poussin's paintings to the French Academy, saying the figures were faithful copies of Roman and Greek statues.

If someone now says 'P's painting is a faithful copy of a Roman statue,' he is not apt to be offering a reason why the work is either good or bad. 'The painting has a touch of blue,' '. . . is a seascape,' '. . . a picture of peasants,' '. . . conforms to the artist's intentions,' '. . . will improve men's morals': these too are not apt to be offered, and if offered cannot be accepted as reasons why the painting is good or bad.

But if someone says 'P's painting is disorganized,' he is apt to be offering a reason why the work is bad (he need not be; this might be part of an answer to 'Which one is P's?'). Even if it is right to say 'P's painting is disorganized,' it may be wrong to conclude 'P's painting is bad,' or even 'P's painting is not good.' Some good paintings are somewhat disorganized; they are good in spite of the fact that

* Originally published in *Philosophy and Education*, ed. I. Scheffler (Boston: Allyn and Bacon, Inc., 1958); reprinted by permission of the publisher.

they are somewhat disorganized. But no painting is good because it is disorganized and many are bad primarily because they are disorganized.

To say 'P's painting is disorganized' may be to offer a good reason why P's painting is bad. It is a consideration. It need not be conclusive. But it is a reason nonetheless. Much the same may be said of reference to the balance, composition, proportions of a painting; but much the same may not be said of certain references to the subject matter, of any reference to the size, shape, effect on morals of a painting. Why is this so? Is this so?

I

Someone might say this: 'If a painting were disorganized and had no redeeming features, one would not call it "a good painting." To understand the relevant uses of the phrase 'a good painting' is to understand, among other things, that to say 'P's painting is disorganized' may be to offer a reason in support of an unfavorable opinion of P's painting.'

This will not do at all even though it is plainly true that someone would not—I would not—call a painting "a good painting" if it were disorganized and had no redeeming features.

Maybe certain persons use the phrase 'a good painting' in such a way that they would call a painting "a good painting" even if it were disorganized and had no redeeming features. Maybe some or even many or most in fact use the phrase 'a good painting' in a way that no painting is good if it is not a seascape. Many people probably use the phrase 'a good painting' in many different ways.

It is true that I and my friends would not call a painting "a good painting" if it were merely disorganized, unredeemed. That is no reason why anyone should accept the fact that a painting is disorganized as a reason in support of an unfavorable opinion of it. To say one would not call it "a good painting" if it were disorganized and had no redeeming features is primarily a way of indicating how strongly one is committed to the acceptance of such a fact as a reason, it is a way of making clear precisely what attitude one has here: it does not show the attitude is reasonable.

Why use the phrase in one way rather than another? Why bother with organization? Why not concentrate on seascapes? on pictures of peasants? Is it merely a linguistic accident that one is concerned with organization? This is not a matter of words. (And this is not to say that the words do not matter: 'That is a good painting' can be queried with 'According to what standards?'; 'That is a magnificent painting' cannot be so queried and neither can 'That is an exquisite painting,' '. . . a splendid painting.')

Only some of the remarks sometimes made while discussing a work of art are reasons in support of a critical evaluation of the work: to evaluate a work one must understand it, appreciate it; much of what is said about a work is directly relevant only to an appreciation of it.

Any fact is relevant to an appreciation of a work if a knowledge of it is likely to facilitate, to enhance, the appreciation of the work. A critic may direct attention to many different facts: the role of the supporting continuo is a central point in Tovey's discussion of Haydn's chamber music. Tovey points out that the supporting continuo was used to fill a crucial gap in the musical structure:

The pioneers of instrumental music in the years 1600–20 showed an accurate instinct by promptly treating all groups of instruments as consisting of a firm bass and a florid treble, held together by an unobtrusive mass of harmony in the middle. Up to the death of Handel and beyond, throughout Haydn's boyhood, this harmonic welding was entrusted to the continuo player, and nobody ever supposed that the polyphony of the "real" orchestral parts could, except accidentally or by way of relief, sound well without this supplement.[1]

When Tovey then says: in the later chamber music Haydn abandoned the use of a supporting continuo, he is saying something of relevance to an appreciation of any one of Haydn's chamber works: who can then listen to an early Haydn quartet and not hear it in a new way? The supporting continuo acquires a new prominence; for a time, an undue prominence in the structure of the whole work. But the end product of this process of re-examining the interrelations of the various parts, to which one has been impelled by the critic's information, is a keener feeling for the texture of the whole.

This is one instance of how historical information can be of value in directing and enlightening the appreciation of a work; there are others. The music of Bach has been compared with that of Schütz, Donne's poetry with that of Cavalcanti, Matisse's work with Egyptian wall paintings. Comparative studies are useful; they provide fresh means of directing and arousing interest in certain aspects of the works under consideration. When a critic shows that work A is intimately related or similar in some important respects to work B, this is of interest not only in that one is then aware of this particular relation between A and B, but more significantly, one may then see both A and B in a different way: A seen in the light of its relation to B can acquire a new lucidity.

Any fact may be relevant to an appreciation of a work, may thereby be indirectly relevant in evaluating it. Presumably every fact directly relevant in evaluating the work is also relevant to an appreciation of it. But the converse is not true, that the work was executed while the artist was in Rome may be relevant to an appreciation of it

[1] D. Tovey, *Essays and Lectures on Music*, pp. 3–4.

but is likely to be relevant in no other way to an evaluation of it. What further requirements must a fact relevant to an appreciation of a work satisfy if it is also to be relevant in evaluating the work?

To say a painting is a good painting is here simply to say it is worth contemplating. (Strictly speaking, this is false but for the time being I am not concerned to speak strictly, but only for the time being. See II below.) Nothing can be a reason why the painting is good unless it is a reason why the painting is worth contemplating. (One can add: for its own sake, but that is redundant.)

Suppose we are in a gallery with a friend looking at P's painting; he somewhat admires the work, is inclined to claim it is good; we wish to deny this, to claim it is a bad painting. We might attempt to support our counter claim by saying 'The painting is clearly disorganized,' offering this as a reason in support of our opinion of the work.

Saying this to him would be a way of drawing his attention to the organization of the painting, to the lack of it, a way of pointing to this aspect of the painting, saying 'Notice this, see the disorder,' not merely this, of course, but at least this.

(Here you see a single great curving diagonal holds together in its sweep nearly everything in the picture. And this diagonal is not built up by forms that are at the same distance from the eye. The forms are arranged so as to lead the eye gradually backwards until we pass out of the stable into the open air beyond. Here . . .[2]

said Roger Fry, discussing a painting by Rubens, focusing the listening eye on the single great curving diagonal, drawing it back and forth across the picture plane, levelling the attention, directing it freely throughout the painting.)

This pointing is a fundamental reason why 'The painting is clearly disorganized' is a reason, and the fact that it is

[2] *French, Flemish and British Art*, p. 125.

indicates why 'The work was executed while the artist was in Rome,' '. . . conforms to the artist's intentions,' '. . . is liked by Bernard,' even though possibly relevant to an appreciation of the work, are not reasons why the painting is good or bad; for all this is not directly relevant. One cannot contemplate the fact that the work was done while the artist was in Rome in the painting; this is not an aspect of the painting, not a characteristic of it which one can either look at or look for. Suppose one were told: 'Notice that the work was done while the artist was in Rome,' one could only reply: 'But what am I supposed to look at?'

Of course one could do this: I say to you 'Think of Rome; then look for things in the picture that will fit in with what you've just been thinking'; you might find a great deal in some pictures, little in others. If I want you to make out a lion in the picture which you seem not to have seen I could say this: 'Remember the work was done in Africa,' 'The artist was much interested in animals.' So it will not do, in one sense, to say that remarks like 'Notice that the work was done while the artist was in Rome' are not reasons because they do not direct or guide one in the contemplation of the work. But in another sense it is obvious that such remarks do not guide or direct one in the contemplation of a work; to suppose that they do is to suppose certain familiar locutions to be signifying in somewhat extraordinary ways.

What is important here is this: one looks at paintings; nothing can be a reason why a painting is good or bad unless it is concerned with what can be looked at in the painting, unless it is concerned with what can, in some sense, be seen.

If it be asked: 'Why insist on this? How does this show that 'The work was done while the artist was in Rome' is not a reason why the painting is good?', a sufficient answer is: only in this way can the reason direct or guide one in the contemplation of the work; a "reason" that failed to do this would not be worth asking for, not worth giving; there would be no reason to be concerned with such a "reason."

But this is not to say that 'The work was done while the artist was in Rome,' '. . . is liked by Bernard,' are necessarily, apart from questions of appreciation, altogether irrelevant; these matters may in many ways be indirectly relevant to an evaluation of a work.

That the work was done while the artist was in Rome, is liked by Bernard, was done in the artist's old age, is detested by people of reputed good taste . . . may be indications, signs, that it is a poor work; these may be very good and important reasons to suppose the work is defective. It is for such reasons as these that one decides not to see a certain exhibition, not to read a certain book, not to hear a certain concert. But such facts as these do not in themselves constitute reasons why the painting is a poor work: indications or signs are never reasons why the painting is good or bad, but at best only reasons to suppose it is good or bad. The fact that C cannot remember D's name is often an indication or a sign of the fact that C dislikes D; it is a reason to suppose C dislikes D; in odd cases it may also be a reason why C dislikes D in that it is a contributing cause of the dislike: an indication or a sign is a reason why only when it is a cause. But one is not here concerned with causes: 'What causes this to be a good painting?' has no literal meaning; 'What makes this a good painting?' asks for a reason why it is a good painting, and this kind of question cannot be answered by citing indications or signs.

This pointing is not the only reason why certain facts are, and others are not, reasons why a painting is good or bad: 'The painting is a seascape' points to a characteristic of the painting, directs one's attention to certain features

53

of the work; for saying this to him could be a way of saying 'Notice this, see that it is a seascape,' yet this is not a reason why the painting is either good or bad.

To say to him 'The painting is a seascape' could be a way of directing his attention to the subject matter of the painting, indicating that the painting was of a certain kind. While contemplating a painting one may consider what kind of work it is, who painted it, what kind of organization it has, what kind of subject matter (if any), what kind of pigmentation. To learn that a painting is by a certain artist, has a certain kind of organization, subject matter, pigmentation, may be relevant to an appreciation of the work; it may enable one to recognize, discern, make out, identify, label, name, classify things in the painting, aspects of the painting; such recognition, identification, classification, may be important in the appreciation of a painting; one who failed to recognize or discern or make out the man in Braque's "Man with a Guitar," the printed letters in a cubist painting, a horse in "Guernica," would be apt to misjudge the balance and organization of these works, would fail to appreciate or understand these works, would be in no position to evaluate them.

That a painting is of a certain kind may be an excellent reason to suppose it is good or bad. But is it ever a reason why the painting is good or bad? Is the fact that the painting is of a certain kind directly relevant to the contemplation of the painting? Does 'The painting is a seascape' direct or guide one in the contemplation of the painting?

Being of a certain kind matters here primarily in connection with the recognition, identification, classification of various elements of the work. Shall we then say: 'Contemplating the subject matter of a painting (or its oganization, or its pigmentation) is not merely a matter of recognizing, identifying, the subject matter, not merely a matter of labelling, naming, classifying'?

That is not enough: it is not that contemplating a painting is not merely a matter of this or that, it is not a matter of recognizing or identifying or classifying or labelling at all.

Contemplating a painting is something one does, something one may be engaged in; one can and does say things like 'I am contemplating this painting,' 'I have been contemplating this painting for some time.' But in this sense, recognizing is not something one does; even though it may be true that while contemplating a painting (which has subject matter) I may recognize, or fail to recognize, or simply not recognize, the subject matter of the painting, it is never true that I am recognizing the subject matter; and this is a way of saying one cannot say 'I am recognizing the subject matter of this painting,' or 'I am recognizing this painting,' or 'I have been recognizing it for some time.'

Recognition is like an event, whereas contemplation is like an activity (much the same may be said of identification or classification in certain relevant senses, though not in all senses, of these terms); certain events may occur during the course of an activity, recognition may or may not take place during the course of contemplation. While contemplating Braque's "Man with a Guitar" one may suddenly (or slowly and at great length) recognize, discern, make out, a figure in the painting; analytical cubistic works often offer such difficulties. If on Monday one recognizes a figure in the Braque painting, on Tuesday there is ordinarily no question of recognition; it has occurred, is over and done with, for the time being; 'I recognize it every time I see it' would be sensible if each time it appeared in a fresh disguise, if I suffered from recurrent amnesia, if it appeared darkly out of a haze. (In the sense in which one can speak of "recognizing" the subject matter of an abstract or semi-abstract work, one often cannot speak of "recognizing" the subject matter of a characteristic

Chardin still-life: one can see, look at, study, examine the apple in the Chardin painting, but there is not likely to be any "recognition.")

This is not to deny that if a work has recognizable elements, recognition may occur during the course of contemplation, nor that if it does occur then the contemplation of the work is, for some people at least, likely to be somewhat enhanced. If recognition is ever a source of delight, that is certainly true; this, too, would be true: the second time one contemplates the work the contemplation of it may be less worthwhile. But whether this is true or not does not really matter here. It appears to be of interest owing only to an ambiguity of 'contemplating.'

'Contemplating' may be employed to refer simply to contemplating, or to someone's contemplation of a work at a certain time and place and under certain conditions. 'In contemplating the work one attends to the organization' is about contemplating, about what one is doing in contemplating the work; to speak of "contemplating a work," or of "the contemplation of a work," is a way of referring only to certain aspects of one's contemplation of a work at a certain time and place and under certain conditions; it is a way of abstracting from considerations of person, place and time. 'In contemplating the work one recognizes a figure in the foreground' is not about contemplating the work; it is not about what one is doing in contemplating the work; it is about something like an event that may occur while someone is contemplating the work for the first or second time under certain conditions. (Contrast 'In walking one's leg muscles are continually being tensed and relaxed' with 'In walking one finds an emerald.')

To say 'Since the work has recognizable elements, recognition is likely to occur while contemplating the work and thus the contemplation of the work will be enhanced' would not be to refer to the contemplation of the work, it would not be to abstract from considerations of time; for it is not the contemplation of the work that would be enhanced, but only and merely the contemplation of the work on that particular occasion when recognition occurred. It is for this reason the fact that the work has recognizable elements—and thus admits of the possibility of recognition occurring during the course of contemplation, so enhancing the contemplation—is not a reason why the work is worth contemplating. To say 'The work is worth contemplating,' or 'Contemplating the work is worthwhile,' is here and ordinarily to speak of contemplating the work, it is here and ordinarily to abstract from considerations of person, place, and time.

Were "Guernica" hung in Hell, contemplating it would hardly be worthwhile, would there be altogether tedious; yet it is not the work that would be at fault, rather the contemplation of the work in the galleries of Hell. But whether this would be the case has no bearing on whether "Guernica" is worth contemplating. It would ordinarily be at best foolish to reply to ' "Guernica" is well worth contemplating' by asking 'When?' or 'Where?' or even 'For whom?' That a certain person, at a certain time and place, finds "Guernica" not worth contemplating may be a slight reason to suppose "Guernica" is not worth contemplating; but it is not a reason why the work is not worth contemplating. If one knows that no one ever has found, or ever will find, "Guernica" worth contemplating, one has excellent reason to suppose "Guernica" is not worth contemplating; one can be absolutely sure it is not worth contemplating; yet this is not even the most trifling reason why "Guernica" is not worth contemplating. This does not ever entitle anyone to say 'I know "Guernica" is not worth contemplating.' All this is but an elaborate way of saying that in saying 'The work is worth contemplating' one is abstracting from considerations of person, place, and time.

What has been said of 'recognition' could be said, in one way or another, of 'identification,' 'classification,' 'labelling,' 'naming'; thus identification, as well as recognition, may occur during the course of contemplation, may enhance the contemplation, is over and done with after a time. But this is never a reason why the painting is good or bad. If recognition, identification, classification, all fail, as they do in fact all fail, to be such a reason, and if nothing can be such a reason unless it is a fact about the work that directs or guides one in the contemplation of the work—thus comparisons or associations are out of order— it follows that the fact that a work is of a certain kind is also incapable of being a reason why the work is worth contemplating. "There can be no objective rule of taste by which what is beautiful may be defined by means of concepts" said Kant,[3] and he was right (but for the wrong reasons).

Let it be clear that nothing has been said to deny that one can be concerned only with recognition, or identification, or classification, or comparisons when contemplating paintings; one can treat a painting in the way an entomologist treats a specimen spider, or be concerned only with puzzle pictures, with conundrums. Nor has it been maintained that to say 'The work is worth contemplating' is necessarily to abstract from considerations of person, place, and time; that this is what is here and ordinarily intended in speaking of "contemplating a painting" is primarily (though not exclusively) a verbal point and does not signify. There are other ways of speaking: A person may choose to say 'The work is worth contemplating' and abstract only from considerations of person, or of place, or of time, or not at all. But if so, he cannot then say what one now wants to say and does say about paintings; for if a person fails or refuses to abstract from such considerations at all, it will be impossible either to agree or disagree

[3] *Critique of Aesthetic Judgement,* I, sec. 17.

with him about the worth of paintings; refusing to abstract from considerations of person, place, and time is tantamount to refusing ever to say, as one now says, 'The work is worth contemplating,' but insisting always on saying things like 'The work is worth contemplating for me, here and now,' or '. . . for him, yesterday, at two o'clock.' One can speak in this way if one chooses; one can do what one wills with paintings. But none of this has anything to do with art.

To state that a painting is a seascape, if it is simply to state that the work is of a certain kind, is not to state a reason why it is good or bad; for that the painting is of a certain kind cannot be such a reason. What can?

Contrast 'The painting is a seascape' with 'The painting is disorganized.' To say the former to someone could be a way of directing his attention to the subject matter of the painting, indicating that it had a certain kind of subject matter; to say the latter not only could but would be a way of directing his attention to the organization of the painting, but it would not be indicating that it had a certain kind of organization.

The sense of 'organization' with which one is here primarily concerned is that in which one can say of any painting 'Notice the organization' without thereby being committed to the view that the painting is in fact organized; one can and does say things like 'The main fault to be found with Pollock's paintings is in the organization: his work is completely disorganized.' (Just so one can on occasion say 'Notice the balance' of a certain painting,' and yet not be committed to saying the painting is balanced.) Every work has an organization in the sense that no matter what arrangement there may be of shapes and shades there is necessarily a particular configuration to be found in the painting. In this sense, the organization is an aspect, a feature, of every painting; something that may be contemplated, studied, and observed, in every painting.

There are various kinds of organization, for the organization of a work is something which may be described, classified, analyzed:

The chief difference between the classical design of Raphael and the Baroque lay in the fact that whilst the artists of the high Renaissance accepted the picture plane and tended to dispose their figures in planes parallel to that—Raphael's cartoons, for instance, almost invariably show this method—the Baroque designers disposed their figures along lines receding from the eye into the depths of the picture space.[4]

'Horizontally, crossing the picture plane,' or 'Primarily rectangular,' or 'Along a single curving diagonal,' could be answers to the question 'What kind of organization does it have?' in a way that 'Organized' or 'Disorganized' could not. 'Organized' and 'Disorganized' are more like states than like kinds of organization ('organized' is more like 'happy' than like 'healthy,' and more like 'healthy' than like 'human').

Yet this is not to deny what cannot be denied, that a sensible answer to 'What kind of painting is it?' might be 'A fairly well organized seascape, somewhat reminiscent of the Maine coast.' 'What kind of painting is it?' is often a request not only to describe the painting, to identify it, name it, classify it, point out its similarities and dissimilarities to other paintings, but also to evaluate the painting, to say whether it is worth bothering with.

But seascapes are a kind of painting in a way disorganized or organized paintings are not; crocodiles are a kind of animal in a way healthy animals are not: unlike 'seascape' and 'crocodile,' 'organized' and 'healthy' admit of questions of degree; one can say 'He is quite healthy,' 'It is somewhat disorganized,' 'It would be less well organized if that were done'; there are and can be no corresponding locutions employing the terms 'seascape'

[4] Fry, *French, Flemish and British Art*, p. 22.

and 'crocodile.' (One could introduce the terms 'seacapish' and 'crocodilish,' but this is to say: one could invent a use for them.) One cannot discriminate between seascapes on the basis of their being seascapes, whereas one can and does discriminate between disorganized paintings on the basis of their being disorganized, for some are more and some are less.

That 'organized,' and 'disorganized,' unlike 'seascape,' admit of questions of degree is important (thus Tolstoi, who knew what art was, and knowing crucified it, spoke of ". . . those infinitely minute degrees of which a work of art consists"[5]); here it indicates that determining whether a painting is disorganized, unlike determining whether it is a seascape, is not a matter of recognition or identification, though it may, on occasion, presuppose such recognition or identification. In order to determine whether a painting is disorganized, it is necessary to contemplate the organization of the painting. To determine whether a painting is a seascape, it is sufficient to recognize or identify the subject matter of the work; it is not necessary to contemplate the subject matter. To say to someone 'The painting is a seascape' could be a way of drawing his attention to the subject matter of the painting, but it would be a way of inviting recognition or identification of certain things in the painting, not a way of inviting contemplation of an aspect of the painting.

'Disorganized,' unlike 'seascape,' reports on an aspect of the painting; one might also say: it refers to a point in a dimension, the particular dimension being that of organization; another point in this dimension is referred to by 'clearly organized,' another by 'an incoherent organization'; to say 'The organization of the painting is defective,' or 'The painting has a defective organization,' or 'The painting is defectively organized,' are ways—different ways—of attributing approximately the same location to the painting

[5] *What is Art?*, p. 201.

61

in the dimension of organization. To say 'The painting is a seascape' is not to direct attention to a certain dimension, that of subject matter; it may direct attention to the subject matter, but not to the dimension of subject matter: such a dimension is found when one considers not the kind but the treatment or handling of subject matter (contrast 'The painting is a seascape' with 'The figures are too stiff, too impassive'); for it does not refer to a point in that dimension; it does not locate the painting in that dimension. (Just so to say 'The painting has a diagonal organization' is not to direct attention to a certain dimension.)

But not any report on any aspect of the painting can be a reason why the painting is good or bad; 'The painting is quite green, predominantly green' reports on an aspect of the painting, yet it is not a reason why the work is good or bad.

To say 'The painting is quite green' could be somewhat like saying 'Notice the organization of the painting' for it could serve to direct attention to an aspect of the painting; but it is not apt to be the relevant kind of report on this aspect. It is not such a report if it does not lead one either to or away from the work: if it were a reason, would it be a reason why the painting is a good painting or a reason why the painting is a bad painting?

But it would not be correct to say it is never a report, in a relevant sense; it is not apt to be, but it might; if someone were to claim that a painting were good and if, when asked why, replied 'Notice the organization!' it could be clear he was claiming that the painting was organized, perhaps superbly organized, that the organization of the work was delightful; just so if he were to claim 'The painting is quite green, predominantly green,' it could be quite clear he was claiming that the greenness of the painting was delightful, that the work was "sufficiently green": 'The painting is quite green' would here be a report on an aspect of the painting, a report leading in one direction. Even so, it is not a reason why the painting is good or bad.

This is not to deny that someone might offer such a statement as the statement of a reason why the painting is good. Nor is it to deny that 'The painting is quite green' has all the marks of such a reason: it points to the painting; it directs one's attention to an aspect of the painting, an aspect that can be contemplated; it reports on this aspect of the painting and thus directs one to the contemplation of the painting. It could be a reason why the painting is good. But it is not. Is it because one simply does not care whether the painting is quite green? because it makes no difference?

One would not ordinarily say to someone 'The painting is clearly disorganized' unless one supposed he had somehow not sufficiently attended to the organization of the work. But more than this. Ordinarily one would not attempt to draw his attention to the organization of the painting, to the lack of it, unless one took for granted that if he did sufficiently attend to the organization and did in fact find the work to be disorganized, he would then realize that the painting was indeed defective.

One sometimes takes for granted that the absence of organization in a painting, once it is attended to, will in fact make much difference to a person; that he will be less inclined and perhaps even cease to find the work worth contemplating. And this is in fact sometimes the case; what one sometimes takes for granted is sometimes so.

This is one reason that a reference to the organization of the work may be a reason, and why a reference to the greenness of the painting is not; one ordinarily neither finds nor takes for granted one will find the fact that the painting is or is not quite green will make any such difference.

Being green or not green is not likely to make any difference to anyone in his contemplation of the painting; but the same is not true of being huge, or of having a sordid

63

subject. Suppose a work were three miles high, two miles long: one simply could not contemplate it; suppose the subject matter of a work were revolting: certainly many could not contemplate it; or again, what if one knew that contemplating a work would have an insidious and evil influence: could one, nonetheless, contemplate it calmly?

There are many factors that may prevent and hinder one from contemplating a work; there are also certain factors that may facilitate the contemplation of a work; figure paintings, the Italian treatment of the figure, Raphael's, Signorelli's, Piero's handling, smoothes the path of contemplation.

Therefore, the nude, and best of all the nude erect and frontal, has through all the ages in our world—the world descended from Egypt and Hellas—been the chief concern of the art of visual representation.[6]

One is inclined to contemplate the nude (though not the naked—there is a difference).

That a painting has revolting subject matter, may seduce the beholder, is too large, too small, does make much difference, but a difference of a different kind..That a painting is too large is in fact a reason why the painting is not good; yet it is a reason of a different kind, for it is also a reason why the painting is not bad: that the painting is too large is not a reason why the contemplation of the work is not worthwhile; rather it is a reason why one cannot contemplate the painting, a reason why one simply cannot evaluate the work.

That a painting is not too large, not too small, is not apt to seduce and is even apt to improve one, has splendid subject matter, are not, in themselves, or in isolation, reasons why a work is a good work, why the work is worth contemplating. Yet such factors as these, by rendering the work accessible to contemplation, can tend to enhance its

[6] Bernard Berenson, *Aesthetics and History*, pp. 81–82.

value. (Memling's "Lady with a Pink" would be less lovely were it larger; "Guernica" would be less majestic were it smaller.) Such factors as these cannot stand alone; alone they are not reasons why the painting is a good painting. That the neighboring woods are nearby does not prove them lovely, but if lovely, then by being nearby they are that much lovelier, and if ugly, that much uglier.

It is here, perhaps, that the locus of greatness, of sublimity, is to be found in art; a painting with a trivial subject, a shoe, a cabbage, may be a superb work, but its range is limited: even if it succeeds, it is not great, not sublime; and if it fails, its failure is of no consequence; it may be trivial, it may be delightful—nothing more. But a figure painting, Signorelli's "Pan," was a great, a sublime painting; had it failed, its failure would have been more tragic than trivial.

Such factors as these often do make a difference, but unlike the fact that the work is well or poorly organized, they do not indicate that the work is or is not worth contemplating: they indicate only that if the work is worth contemplating, it will be well worth contemplating; and if it is not worth contemplating, then possibly it will be not merely not worth contemplating, but distressing.

One sometimes takes for granted that the presence or absence of organization will make a difference to the person. But what if it does not?

It is quite possible that it will not. It is possible that to some people it makes no difference at all whether a painting is disorganized. It may even be that some people prefer what are in fact disorganized paintings (though they might not call them "disorganized"). Perhaps some people greatly admire quite green paintings; the fact that a painting is or is not quite green will make much difference to them.

Someone might now want to say this: 'Even though you may happen to like a disorganized painting at a time, you won't like it after a time; disorganized paintings do not wear well.' Or this: 'Even though you may happen to like a disorganized painting, your liking of it will interfere with and narrow the range of your appreciation of many other paintings.' Or even this: 'Your liking of it is unlike that of someone who likes an organized painting; for such a person will not only like it longer, but will like it in a different and better way: "not merely a difference in quantity, but a difference in quality." Thus the satisfaction, the value, he finds in contemplating an organized painting is unlike and better than that you find in contemplating a disorganized painting.'

It is sometimes true that disorganized paintings do not wear well, but it sometimes is not true; some people persist in liking unlikable paintings. Will perseverance do to transmute vice to virtue? It is sometimes true that a taste for disorganized paintings is apt to interfere with and narrow the range of one's appreciations of other paintings; but is it not likely that one who likes both organized and disorganized paintings will have the more catholic taste? Is it wise to be a connoisseur of wine and cut one's self off from the pleasures of the poor? There is a sense in which it is certainly true that the satisfaction one finds in contemplating an organized painting is unlike and superior to that one finds in contemplating a disorganized painting, but in the sense in which it is, it is here irrelevant: for of course it is certainly true that the satisfaction and value found in connection with a good painting is superior to that found in connection with a bad painting—this of course being a necessary statement. But apart from the fact that the satisfaction found in connection with a good painting is of course superior to that found in connection with a bad painting, what reason is there to suppose in fact—and not merely of course—this is the case? I find no satisfaction in connection with a bad painting, so how shall I compare to see which is superior?

66

One sometimes says: 'Last year I found satisfaction in connection with what I now see to be a bad painting. Now I can see that my satisfaction then was inferior to my satisfaction now found in connection with a good painting.' So you might predict to someone: 'Just wait! Cultivate your taste and you will see that the satisfaction found in connection with good-A will be superior to the satisfaction, value, you now find in connection with bad-B.'

And what if he does not? (Is it not clear that here aesthetics has nothing to do with consequences?) A man might say: 'I find the very same kind of satisfaction in this "disorganized" painting that you find in that "organized" one: I too am greatly moved, greatly stirred. You may say of course your satisfaction, the value you find, is superior to mine; in fact it is not.' He might be lying, but could he be mistaken?

There is then an inclination to say this: 'If being organized or being disorganized does make much difference to a person then for him it is a reason, whereas if it does not make any such difference, it is not.' This would be to say that instead of speaking of "the reasons why the painting is good," one would have to speak of "his reasons why" and "my reasons why" and "your reasons why" if one wished to speak precisely. This will not do at all.

I or you or he can have a reason to suppose (think, believe) the work is worth contemplating; but neither I nor you nor he can have a reason why the work is worth contemplating; anyone may know such a reason, discover, search for, find, wonder about such a reason, but no one can ever have such a reason; even when one has found such a reason, one can only point to it, present it, never appropriate it for one's own; 'What are your reasons?' makes sense in reply to 'I believe it is worth contemplating,' but it has no literal sense if asked of 'I know it is worth contemplating.' 'My reasons why the work is worth contemplating

67

. . . ,' 'The reason for me the work is worth contemplating . . . ,' are also here without relevant literal meaning.

(It would be absurd to describe this fact by saying that what is a reason for me must be a reason for everyone else— as though what no one ever could own must therefore be owned by all alike. What one could say here is that a reason must be as abstract as the judgment it supports.)

If being organized or being disorganized does make much difference to a person then, not "for him" nor "in that case," nor "then and there," it is apt to be a reason; for in that case, then and there, one can forget about him then and there; whereas if it does not make any such difference then, for him, in that case, then and there, it is not apt to be a reason, for in that case, then and there, one cannot forget about him then and there.

To say 'The work is worth contemplating' is here and ordinarily to abstract from considerations of person; but such abstraction is, as it were, a minor achievement, an accomplishment possible only when there either is or can be a community of interest. I can ignore the ground I walk on so long as it does not quake. This fact cannot be ignored: contemplating a painting is something that people do, different people.

Paradise gardens are not ever simply a place (one could not be there not knowing it, and it is in part because I know I am not there that I am not there); not being simply a place, paradise gardens are proportioned to everyman's need, even though these requirements may at times be incompatible. But these lesser perfections that paintings are are less adaptable, answer only to some men's need.

Reasoning about works of art is primarily a social affair, an attempt to build and map our common Eden; it can be carried on fruitfully only so long as there is either a common care or the possibility of one. But Kant was wrong in saying aesthetic judgments presuppose a common sense:

one cannot sensibly presuppose what is often not the case. A community of interest and taste is not something given, but something that can be striven for.

II

And now I can be more precise, and that is to say, more general, for we speak of "good poems," "good quartets," "good operas," as well as "good paintings." But the problem is always the same. A good anything is something that answers to interests associated with it. In art, this is always a matter of performing certain actions, looking, listening, reading, in connection with certain spatio-temporal or temporal entities, with paintings, poems, musical compositions.

Formulaically, there is only this: A person p_i, performs an action, a_i, in connection with an entity, e_i, under conditions, c_i; George contemplates Fouquet's "Madonna" in the gallery at Antwerp; e_i is good if and only if the performance of the relevant a_i by p_i under c_i is worthwhile for its own sake. To state a reason why e_i is good is simply to state a fact about e_i in virtue of which the performance of the relevant a_i by p_i under c_i is worthwhile for its own sake.

Someone says, pointing to a painting, 'That is a good painting.' There is (at least) a triple abstraction here, for neither the relevant persons, nor actions, nor conditions, have been specified. Is it any wonder we so often disagree about what is or is not a good painting?

Persons: George and Josef disagree about a Breughel. Say Josef is color-blind. Then here I discount Josef's opinion: I am not color-blind. But if they were concerned with a Chinese ink drawing, color-blindness could be irrelevant. George is not a peasant, neither does he look kindly on peasants, not even a Breughel painting of peasants. Well, neither do I, so I would not, for that reason, discount his opinion. Josef is a prude, that is, a moralist, and he looks uncomfortably at the belly of a Titian nude. I would discount his opinion, for I am not. (This is why it is horrible nonsense to talk about "a competent observer" in matters of art appreciation: no one is competent or not competent to look at the belly of a Titian nude.) But George has no stomach for George Grosz's pictures of butchers chopping up pigs, and neither do I, so I would not discount his opinion there. George has a horror of churches: his opinion of stained glass may be worthless. Not having an Oedipus complex, George's attitude toward "Whistler's Mother" is also eccentric. And so on.

If e_i is good then the performance of a_i by p_i under c_i is worthwhile for its own sake. But this obviously depends on the physical, psychological, and intellectual, characteristics of p_i. If p_i and p_j are considering a certain work then the relevant characteristics of p_i depend on the particular p_j, e_i, a_i, and c_i involved. It is worse than useless to stipulate that p_i be "normal": what is that to me if I am not normal? and who is? To be normal is not necessary in connection with some limited works, and it is not enough to read *Finnegan's Wake*. Different works make different demands on the person. The popularity of "popular art" is simply due to the fact that it demands virtually nothing: one can be as ignorant and brutish as a savage and still deal with it.

But there is no point in worrying about persons for practically nothing can be done about them. Actions are what matter. Art education is a matter of altering the person's actions, and so, conceivably, the person.

Actions: Here we have a want of words. Aestheticians are fond of 'contemplate,' but one cannot contemplate an opera, a ballet, a cinema, a poem. Neither is it sensible to contemplate just any painting, for not every painting lends itself to contemplation. There is only one significant problem in aesthetics, and it is not one that an aesthetician can answer: given a work e_i under conditions c_i, what are the relevant a_i? An aesthetician cannot answer the question because it depends on the particular e_i and c_i: no general answer exists.

Roughly speaking, I survey a Tintoretto, while I scan an H. Bosch. Thus I step back to look at the Tintoretto, up to look at the Bosch. Different actions are involved. Do you drink brandy in the way you drink beer? Do you drive a Jaguar XKSS in the way you drive a hearse?

A generic term will be useful here: 'aspection,' to aspect a painting is to look at it in some way. Thus to contemplate a painting is to perform one act of aspection; to scan it is to perform another; to study, observe, survey, inspect, examine, scrutinize, are still other acts of aspection. There are about three hundred words available here in English, but that is not enough.

Generally speaking, a different act of aspection is performed in connection with works belonging to different schools of art, which is why the classification of style is of the essence. Venetian paintings lend themselves to an act of aspection involving attention to balanced masses; contours are of no importance, for they are scarcely to be found. The Florentine school demands attention to contours, the linear style predominates. Look for light in a Claude, for color in a Bonnard, for contoured volumes in a Signorelli.

George and Josef are looking at Van der Weyden's "Descent from the Cross." Josef complains 'The figures seem stiff, the Christ unnatural.' George replies 'Perhaps. But notice the volumes of the heads, the articulation of the planes, the profound movement of the contours.' They are not looking at the painting in the same way, they are performing different acts of aspection.

They are looking at the "Unicorn Tapestry." Josef complains 'But the organization is so loose!' So Spenser's great *Faerie Queene* is ignored because fools try to read it as though it were a sonnet of Donne, for the *Queene* is a medieval tapestry, and one wanders about in it. An epic is not an epigram.

George says 'A good apple is sour' and Josef says 'A good apple is sweet,' but George means a cooking apple, Josef

71

means a desert apple. So one might speak of "a scanning-painting," "a surveying-painting," and just so one speaks of "a Venetian painting," "a sonata," "a lyric poem," "an improvisation."

If e_i is good then the performance of a_i by p_i under c_i is worthwhile for its own sake. If p_i performs a_i under c_i in connection with e_i, whereas p_j performs a_j under c_i in connection with e_i, p_i and p_j might just as well be looking at two different paintings (or poems). It is possible that the performance of a_i under c_i in connection with e_i is worthwhile for its own sake, while the performance of a_j under c_i in connection with e_i is not worthwhile for its own sake.

There is no easy formula for the relevant actions. Many are possible: only some will prove worthwhile. We find them by trial and error. The relevant actions are those that prove worthwhile in connection with the particular work, but we must discover what these are.

Imagine that "Guernica" had been painted in the time of Poussin. Or a Mondrian. What could the people of the time have done with these works? The question the public is never tired of asking is: 'What am I to look at? look for?' and that is to say: what act of aspection is to be performed in connection with e_i?

Before 1900, El Greco was accredited a second-rate hack whose paintings were distorted because he was blind in one eye. Who bothered with Catalonian frescoes? The Pompeian murals were buried.

Modern art recreates the art of the past, for it teaches the critics (who have the ear of museum and gallery directors who pick the paintings the public consents to see) what to look for and at in modern works. Having been taught to look at things in a new way, when they look to the past, they usually find much worth looking at, in this new way, that had been ignored. So one could almost say that Lehmbruck did the portal of Chartres, Daumier gave birth to

Hogarth, and someone (unfortunately) did Raphael in.

Artists teach us to look at the world in new ways. Look at a Mondrian, then look at the world as though it were a Mondrian and you will see what I mean. To do this, you must know how to look at a Mondrian.

And now I can explain why a reason why a work is good or bad is worth listening to. One reason why a (good) Mondrian is good is that it is completely flat. If that sounds queer to you, it is because you do not know how to look at a Mondrian. And that is why the reason is worth considering.

A reason why e_i is good is a fact about e_i in virtue of which the performance of a_i by p_i under c_i is worthwhile for its own sake. So I am saying that the fact that the Mondrian is completely flat indicates that the performance of a_i by p_i under c_i is worthwhile in connection with the Mondrian painting. In telling you this, I am telling you something about the act of aspection to be performed in connection with the work, for now you know at least this: you are to look at the work spatially, three-dimensionally. (Without the painting to point to, I can only give hints: Look at it upside down! Right side up, each backward movement into space is counterbalanced by an advancing movement. The result is a tense, dynamic, and dramatic picture plane held intact by the interplay of forces. Turn the painting upside down and the spatial balance is detroyed: the thing is hideous.)

Reasons in criticism are worthwhile because they tell us what to do with the work, and that is worth knowing. Yao Tsui said:

It may seem easy for a man to follow the footsteps of his predecessors, but he does not know how difficult it is to follow the movements of curved lines. Although one may chance to measure the speed of the wind which blows through the Hsiang valley, he may have difficulty in fathoming the watercourses of the Lü-liang mountain. Although one may make a good beginning by the skilful use of instruments, yet the ultimate meaning of an object may remain obscure to him until the end. Without knowing the song completely, it is useless to crave for the response of the falling dust.

IV

On What a Painting

Represents*

IF a painting P is a representation of something a, what makes P a representation of a?

1. A straightforward view is this: P is a representation of a if and only if there is a certain correspondence between P and a. Thus, if P is a representation of a house, elements of P correspond to elements of a house and certain relations between the relevant elements of P correspond to certain relations between the relevant elements of the house.

Even if this view were correct it would be irrelevant here. There is a difference between a painting and a blueprint: a blueprint may constitute a structural representation of a house whereas a painting may be a pictorial representation of a house. We are here concerned with paintings. Hence our question is: If P is a pictorial representation of a, what makes P a pictorial representation of a?

2. An answer is: P is a pictorial representation of a if

* Presented in a symposium on "Aesthetics" at the fifty-seventh annual meeting of the American Philosophical Association, Eastern Division, December 27, 1960; originally published in *The Journal of Philosophy*, LVII (1960); reprinted by permission.

and only if there is a certain correspondence between P and a visual aspect of a.

This must be mistaken. Some paintings provide pictorial representations of unicorns but unicorns do not exist and hence have no visual aspect to correspond to.

3. Then say P is a pictorial representation of a if and only if there is a certain correspondence between P and either an actual visual aspect of a or a visual aspect a would have were it to exist or occur. ('Occur' is required here, for there are pictorial representations of mythical events: events do not "exist," they occur.) Thus one may paint a picture of the house one intends to build, and, if one were to build it accordingly, the house would then have a visual aspect to which the painting corresponds.

But then all paintings would be representational. For one could construct something having a visual aspect such that the requisite correspondence obtained between some non-objective painting and a visual aspect of it. Let k be an imaginary thing such that if it were to exist it would have a visual aspect to which some nonobjective painting corresponds. Then the nonobjective painting in question is a pictorial representation of k since it corresponds to a visual aspect k would have were it to exist.

4. And now some may be inclined to say this: P is a pictorial representation of a if and only if there is a certain actual and intended correspondence between P and either an actual visual aspect of a or a visual aspect a would have were it to exist or occur.

Then even if a certain painting looks remarkably like a photograph of a horse, if the correspondence between the painting and a visual aspect of a horse was not intended then the painting is not a pictorial representation of a horse.

It also follows that a painting P pictorially representing a could look exactly like a painting Q pictorially representing b and yet P might not represent b and Q not represent a. The reason why this is so is simply this: According to this view, in order for a pictorial representation of *a* to look exactly like a pictorial representation of *b* it is necessary only that *a* and *b* have a single momentary visual aspect in common. Thus a photograph of a man smiling could look exactly like a photograph of the man grimacing even though a motion picture of the man smiling would not look like a motion picture of the man grimacing.

5. Suppose George paints a painting P which is intended to and which does correspond to a visual aspect of a man leaning against a slender tree trunk with one arm around the trunk. The man's hand and shoulder are visible but not the arm joining the hand and shoulder, for that is behind the trunk.

Suppose Josef paints a painting Q which looks exactly like P, but Q, unlike P, is intended to and does correspond to a visual aspect of a one-armed man leaning against a slender tree trunk on which his severed hand has been fixed in such a way as to look the way it would look if it were unsevered from his arm and his arm were around the trunk.

Then even though P and Q look exactly alike, we must say that in P an unsevered hand is represented whereas in Q a severed hand is represented. Furthermore, insofar as an unsevered hand is represented in P, P may have a commonplace character, whereas insofar as a severed hand is represented in Q, Q may have a bizarre character. But if so, P may be commonplace while Q is bizarre even though they look exactly alike, and that is absurd.

6. If P and Q look exactly alike, then P is a pictorial representation of *a* if and only if Q is a pictorial representation of *a*.

But suppose George and Josef are identical twins, that I am fond of George but not of Josef, that I commission an artist to do a painting of George, and that I then hang the painting of George on my wall. If someone asks me why I have a painting of Josef on my wall when I do not like Josef, the answer is that the painting is not a painting of Josef, it is a painting of George. Furthermore, even if the artist were then to do a painting of Josef and that painting were to look exactly like the painting of George, it would be a painting of Josef, not of George.

7. What this indicates is not that P and Q may look exactly alike and yet be pictorial representations of different things; it indicates that we must distinguish between the question what a painting is a painting of and the question what a painting is a pictorial representation of.

That the painting of George is a painting of George and not of Josef is primarily owing to the fact that the painting was intended to correspond to a visual aspect of George. That it happens also to correspond to a visual aspect of Josef is, as it were, an accident. And if it so happened that the painting of George looked more like Mack than like George himself, the painting would nonetheless be a painting of George and not of Mack. Thus Braque's "Man With A Guitar" is a painting of a man with a guitar though it does not look like a man with a guitar.

8. But if it is true that if P and Q look exactly alike then P is a pictorial representation of a if and only if Q is a pictorial representation of a, then an intended correspondence cannot be required. The term 'intended' is too strong.

Then suppose we say this: P is a pictorial representation of a if and only if P looks as if it were intended to correspond and does in fact correspond in a certain way to either an actual visual aspect of a or a visual aspect a would have were it to exist or occur.

So, if a certain painting looks remarkably like a photograph of a horse and if it looks—as presumably it would look—as if it were intended to correspond to a visual aspect of a horse, then, no matter what the artist's intentions were, it is a pictorial representation of a horse.

And so Josef's painting is a pictorial representation of a man with his arm around a tree and not, as Josef intended, a one-armed man leaning against a tree on which his severed

78

hand has been fixed in such a way as to look the way it would look if it were unsevered from his arm and his arm were around the tree. For Josef's painting would not look as if it were intended to correspond to such a visual aspect of a one-armed man. (This is not to deny that Josef's painting could be seen as representing a one-armed man. One who knew what the painting was a painting of might see it in that way. A painting can be seen as representing something that it is not in fact a pictorial representation of.)

9. But how on this view is it possible for a painting to be a pictorial representation of something completely unfamiliar?

Suppose an artist were to represent certain bacilli seen on looking through a microscope. To a person completely unfamiliar with the visual aspects of bacilli such a painting might not look as if it were intended to correspond to anything. But to one familiar with the visual aspects of bacilli the painting presumably would look as if it were intended to correspond to one of them.

Presumably it is possible for a painting to be a pictorial representation of something completely unfamiliar. So the view under consideration is mistaken.

10. Then suppose we say this: P is a pictorial representation of a if and only if, first, P corresponds in a certain way to either an actual visual aspect of a or a visual aspect a would have were it to exist or occur, and, secondly, to a normal person reasonably familiar with the actual visual aspects of a or with the visual aspects a would have were it to exist or occur, P looks as if it were intended to correspond to either an actual visual aspect of a or a visual aspect a would have were it to exist or occur.

That the concept of familiarity should be relevant in connection with the concept of representation need not be surprising. It is suggested by the morphological structure of the word 'represent.'

But then again all paintings must be representational.

For one could construct something k having a visual aspect such that the requisite correspondence obtained between some non-objective painting and a visual aspect of k. Consequently, to a normal person reasonably familiar with the visual aspects k would have were it to exist, the nonobjective painting would look as if it were intended to correspond to a visual aspect k would have were it to exist. Since the painting does in fact correspond to a visual aspect k would have were it to exist, on this view the nonobjective painting must be a pictorial representation of k.

11. Intuitively speaking, one is inclined to say that P is a pictorial representation of a if and only if P in some sense represents a, thus only if P in some sense "presents" a again. Yet, oddly enough, paintings can represent the completely unfamiliar, something never before "presented," and something that neither does nor ever did exist. So the problem is: If unfamiliar bacilli and nonexistent unicorns can be pictorially represented, why not the unfamiliar nonexistent k?

And an answer is: because it is both unfamiliar and nonexistent. Apart from any painting representing a unicorn, some of us have a fairly good idea what a unicorn would look like if there were any unicorns. But apart from the nonobjective painting in question, none of us has any idea what k would look like if it existed.

Unfamiliar bacilli can be represented pictorially because they have visual aspects to which a painting could correspond. Unicorns can be represented pictorially but not simply because they would have visual aspects if they existed. They can be represented pictorially because certain specifiable visual aspects are attributed to unicorns. Unlike unfamiliar bacilli, k is nonexistent, and, unlike unicorns, no specifiable visual aspects are attributed to k.

12. So suppose we say this: P is a pictorial representation of a if and only if, first, P corresponds in a certain way to either an actual visual aspect of a or a specifiable visual

aspect attributed to *a*, and, secondly, to a normal person reasonably familiar with the actual visual aspects of *a* or with the specifiable visual aspects attributed to *a*, P looks as if it were intended to correspond to either an actual visual aspect of *a* or a specifiable visual aspect attributed to *a*.

And though this approximates to a plausible view, it is still mistaken: all talk of *P*'s looking as if it were intended to correspond to something is perhaps close to but nonetheless beside the point.

13. In deciding that Josef's painting of a one-armed man is not in fact a pictorial representation of a one-armed man, one does not in fact consider whether or not the painting looks as if it were intended to correspond to a visual aspect of a one-armed man.

For suppose the painting were signed by Josef, and in a bold hand, and suppose it were a well-known fact that Josef was fond of painting one-armed men and that he intended his paintings to represent one-armed men but, stupidly enough, he tended to paint one-armed men in such a way as to make them look like two-armed men. Then to one who knew this the painting would look as if it were intended to correspond to a visual aspect of a one-armed man. Even so, the painting would not be a pictorial representation of a one-armed man.

What is important here is not the intention of the artist but something else.

14. The problem of Josef's painting can be posed as follows. Let *a* be a two-armed man, let *b* be a one-armed man with an adjacent severed hand. Then *a* has a set of visual aspects {*a*} associated with it, where the members of {*a*} are either the actual visual aspects of *a* or specifiable visual aspects attributed to *a*; just so, *b* has a set of visual aspects {*b*} associated with it. There is a visual aspect *c* such that Josef's painting Q corresponds to *c* in a relevant way and such that *c* is a member both of {*a*} and of {*b*}. If we say that Q is a pictorial representation of *a* but not of *b* then

we are saying that even though c is a member both of $\{a\}$ and of $\{b\}$, for some reason c is here associated with a. The question is: why?

An answer is this: Such a sight of a two-armed man is familiar; such a sight of a one-armed man with an adjacent severed hand is unfamilar, rare. Thus the probability that c occur in connection with a is greater than the probability that c occur in connection with b.

So let us say this: P is a pictorial representation of a if and only if, first, a has associated with it a set of visual aspects $\{a\}$ such that the members of this set are either actual visual aspects of a or specifiable visual aspects attributed to a, secondly, there is either an actual or specifiable visual aspect c such that P corresponds in the relevant way to c, thirdly, c is a member of $\{a\}$, and, fourthly, if there is a b such that b has a set of visual aspects $\{b\}$ associated with it, b is not identical with a, $\{b\}$ is not identical with $\{a\}$, and c is a member both of $\{a\}$ and of $\{b\}$, then the probability that c be associated with a must be equal to or greater than the probability that c be associated with b.

15. But suppose the question is raised whether a representation of a man in riding boots is a representation of a web-footed man in riding boots or a representation of a nonweb-footed man in riding boots, and suppose that the painting corresponds to a visual aspect c such that c is a member both of the set of visual aspects associated with a web-footed man in riding boots and of the set of visual aspects associated with a nonweb-footed man in riding boots. Then, according to this view, the painting is a representation of a nonweb-footed man in riding boots, for that is the more probable thing.

Yet is it not more reasonable to say that the painting is simply a representation of a man in riding boots? Thus the painting is neither a representation of a nonweb-footed man nor a representation of a web-footed man in riding boots.

If one sees a man in riding boots, then either the man is web-footed or nonweb-footed: he must be one or the other; conceivably one could get him to take off his boots and so settle the matter. But that is one difference between a man in riding boots and a representation of a man in riding boots. Unlike a real man in riding boots, a representation of a man in riding boots might be simply that.

16. The case of the representation of the man leaning against the tree and the case of the representation of the man in riding boots are not alike. In each case, there is a visual aspect c such that c is a member both of the set of visual aspects associated with a and of a set associated with b. But the difference is this: In the former case the relevant sets $\{a\}$ and $\{b\}$ are markedly dissimilar whereas in the latter case the relevant sets $\{a\}$ and $\{b\}$ are identical. Thus, other things being equal, a one-armed man leaning against a tree on which a severed hand is fixed may not look the same as a two-armed man leaning against the tree with one arm around the trunk. But, other things being equal, a web-footed man in riding boots looks the same as a nonweb-footed man in riding boots.

I suggest that a reasonably adequate answer to our question, then, is this: P is a pictorial representation of a if and only if, first, a has associated with it a set of visual aspects $\{a\}$ such that the members of this set are either actual visual aspects of a or specifiable visual aspects attributed to a, secondly, there is either an actual or a specifiable visual aspect c such that P corresponds in a relevant way to c, thirdly, c is a member of $\{a\}$, fourthly, if there is a b such that b has a set of visual aspects $\{b\}$ associated with it, b is not identical with a, $\{b\}$ is not identical with $\{a\}$, and c is a member both of $\{a\}$ and of $\{b\}$, then the probability that c be associated with a must be equal to or greater than the probability that c be associated with b, and fifthly, there is no b having associated with it a set of visual aspects $\{b\}$

such that {a} is identical with {b} but b is not identical with a.

At the moment this seems to me to be a plausible characterization of pictorial representation. But I shall not be surprised if in a few moments it seems otherwise.

V

"Truth and Poetry"

1. O the moon shone bright on Mrs. Porter
    And on her daughter
    They wash their feet in soda water

That is what Eliot said. Is it true?

I will tell you another story. (It is called a "koan.") A monk asked Fuketsu: "Without speaking, without silence, how can you express the truth?" Fuketsu observed: "I remember spring in southern China. The birds sing among many flowers." There is a comment on this koan by the Zen master Mumon. Mumon said: "Fuketsu used to have lightning Zen. Whenever he had the opportunity, he flashed it. But this time he failed to do so and only borrowed from an old Chinese poem. Never mind Fuketsu's Zen. If you want to express the truth, throw out your words, throw out your silence, and tell me about your own Zen."

2. The heavens rejoyce in motion, why should I
    Abjure my so much lov'd variety,
    And not with many youth and love divide?
    Pleasure is none, if not diversifi'd:

That is what Donne said. "Pleasure is none, if not diversifi'd": is that a true statement?

To make a statement is to perform a certain speech act. So one utters a certain utterance in an appropriate way and under appropriate conditions. Reciting a poem and making a statement are not the same.

Is the statement that "pleasure is none, if not diversifi'd" true? Donne said: "Pleasure is none, if not diversifi'd" but he was not making a statement: he was writing a poem. 'Wash your feet in soda water!' can be an order. I have not given you an order. I am not in a position to do so. I have given you an example of an order. The order 'Wash your feet in soda water!' would be a foolish order. It does not follow that I have done anything foolish here. Giving an example of an order and writing a poem are not much alike. Yet they are this much alike: to give an example of an order is not to give an order and to write a poem is not to make a statement.

3. Why bother with the difficult word 'statement'? If I say that it is raining, am I making a statement? Or if I say that I grow weary of the vagaries of aesthetics, am I making a statement? I think not. We could pin the word down but it is not worth the effort.

Donne says that "pleasure is none, if not diversifi'd"; is what he says true? The words "Pleasure is none, if not diversifi'd" occur in Donne's *Elegie* XVII: it does not follow that Donne said that pleasure is none, if not diversifi'd. I say it is not true that Chapman is not worth reading and now it is true that I have said 'Chapman is not worth reading' but it is not true that I have said that Chapman is not worth reading. On the contrary, I said the contradictory.

4. What does Donne say?

> The heavens rejoyce in motion, why should I
> Abjure my so much lov'd variety,
> And not with many youth and love divide?

Does Donne say that he should "abjure . . . variety"? To whom does "I" refer?

> By childrens births, and death, I am become
> so dry, that I am now mine owne sad tombe.

It is not Donne but Niobe who has become her "owne sad tombe." The variable lover asks why he should "abjure . . . variety": that this variable ranges over Donne is not stated. Does it matter who is speaking? What matters is whether or not it is said by someone in the poem that "pleasure is none, if not diversifi'd." But the sense of what is said depends on who says it and when and why: this is generally so so why not in poems?

5. Then the youthful lover asks why he should "abjure . . . variety" and it is he who says that "pleasure is none, if not diversifi'd." Is what he says true?

It is a youthful lover, yes ("with many youth and love divide") but more than that, one who loves variety ("my so much lov'd variety").

Then is it true that for one who is youthful and loves variety, "pleasure is none, if not diversifi'd"?

(Why not read the poem, even the few lines quoted?) There is a question; "why should I / Abjure my so much lov'd variety / And not with many youth and love divide?" So there is the suggestion that the youthful lover should "abjure" his "so much lov'd variety." And it is in opposition to and in contrast with this suggestion that it is said that "pleasure is none, if not diversifi'd."

If I simply say 'Pleasure is none, if not diversifi'd,' I may be talking about pleasure, only about pleasure. I may imply nothing much. But if I am urged to abjure a variety of loves and I reply 'Pleasure is none, if not diversifi'd,' that is another matter. For then there is the implication that love is for pleasure.

6. Is not this a prolonged quibble? No doubt it is difficult to pin down Donne and say that just this or that is said in the *Elegie*. Even so, sooner or later one is done and can say what is said and then ask: is that true?

87

Is what true?

We can simplify matters by supposing that the *Elegie* consists of only the four lines quoted: a poet could have written just such a four line poem. And our problem is "truth and poetry," not this or that particular poem. So we can suppose that Donne wrote only the four lines quoted: that is the whole poem. Then it should be less difficult to say what is said.

7. But Donne is always double dealing. The suggestion is that the youthful lover should "abjure" his "much lov'd variety." The reply appears to be that "pleasure is none, if not diversifi'd," thus implying that love is for pleasure and pleasure demands diversity, variety. Thus a glib hedonistic note is struck. Why should I do this or that? Pleasure is the answer. But is it?

"The heavens rejoyce in motion": the heavens are in motion and the movement of the sun is a form of rejoicing. Motion is in accordance with the order of the universe. And the heavens "rejoyce" in, take delight in, approve of motion, which is to say change, variety. If it is already known that what I do is in accordance with the order of the heavens and will accord the heavens delight, and if in reply to the suggestion that I should abjure doing this I say that pleasure is none, if not diversifi'd, you cannot justly accuse me of being a simple hedonist. For I have not said that the answer to the question why I should do this or that is simply pleasure.

"Why should I / Abjure my so much lov'd variety": here a mock moral note is sounded. To "abjure" is to forswear and why should I forswear and so be false to "my so much lov'd variety," which is to say be false to my many loves? "And not with many youth and love divide?": what is fairer than an equitable distribution? And there is enough for all: "my so much lov'd variety," each is "so much lov'd." "Pleasure is none, if not diversifi'd," which

88

may be to say not only that pleasure requires variety but that unless many have pleasure, none have.

The tone is light. The reply "Pleasure is none, if not diversifi'd" is a mock reply. The supporting "argument" is a mock argument verging on paradox. Why should I be false to my many loves? Yet being true to two is being false to both.

Is what Donne says true?

8. I read a child a story and I say "Once upon a time there was an old woman who lived in a shoe. . . ." The child asks "Was there really?" and I say "No, this is just a story."

If I say to a woman:

> Had we but world enough and time
> This coyness, Lady, were no crime

and she asks "Is that true?," then she is stupid.

Or maybe I am stupid and she is as deep as a well.

There are ways of looking at things and one way is to ask while looking 'Is it true?.' If I look at a billiard table and ask myself 'Is the cloth true?,' I look at the cloth in a certain way. Suppose I take that billiard cloth and make myself a coat and then ask myself 'Is the cloth true?,' what am I to say?

I say "a little nonsense now and Zen"[1] is a fine thing but how do you read a poem?

9. Compare

> Long lines of cliff breaking have left a chasm;

with

> Stand still, and I will read to thee,

—the first is the opening line of Tennyson's *Enoch Arden*, the second of Donne's *A Lecture upon the Shadow*. Here, out of context, how do you read them?

[1] From a conversation with H. D. Aiken.

Do I mean with feeling, in a loud or soft voice? That is not to the point. What do you do in reading them?

I look at the printed page. I read from left to right. That is what I do.

But that is not all I do or anyone does in reading anything. For at least anyone may or may not pay attention to what he is reading and he may do this in different ways and he may attend to different things.

In reading the line of Tennyson's you attend to the movement of the line. Of course you do not choose to do so. If you can read at all, you cannot help being caught up in its movement. You hardly have to listen for the line's echo: if you can read you will hear it. But what one does not do is attend to the words in Tennyson's line in the way one can and must attend to the words in the line from Donne.

"Long lines of cliff . . .": what about "long lines"? Nothing, nothing at all. "Long lines" doesn't matter, just "long lines of cliff." You cannot take the phrase apart or rather if you do it will then be apart, nothing more. Nothing follows. To see that that is so you must of course read the rest of *Enoch Arden*. But you will see that that is so.

"Stand still, and I will read to thee": why "stand still"? Why "still"? And in Donne there is (always?) an answer. For love is likened to the sun at "noone" and "Except our loves at this noone stay," love will decay. So bid the sun stand still! And why "read"? "A Lecture, Love, in loves philosophy": so one reads philosophy (in the English sense, reading law at an Inn) to take a degree: "That love hath not attain'd the highest degree / Which is still diligent lest others see."

'How does one read a poem?' has no one answer. There is no one way of reading a poem. It depends on all sorts of factors but above all on the poem. Anyone who reads a lyric as though it were a metaphysical sonnet is as much

a fool as a man who swigs brandy and sips beer. Words-
worth is no Marvell but you will not find even what is
worth finding if you read *Tintern Abbey* as though it were
The Garden.

10. "O the moon shone bright on Mrs. Porter": If I
ask myself 'Is that true?,' what am I supposed to be asking?

If I knew a Mrs. Diana Porter who was shot in the head
while hunting at night, I might wonder how anyone could
see where to shoot. If someone said that the moon shone
bright on Mrs. Porter then if I asked myself 'Is that true?,'
I would know what sort of question I was asking.

If we were looking at a newspaper account of the
slaughter of Mrs. Porter and it said 'The moon shone
bright on Mrs. Porter,' I should not be appalled by the
question 'Is that true?.' But if we are reading Eliot and
some adult points to the line "O the moon shone bright
on Mrs. Porter" and asks 'Is that true?' then I think that
person is stupid.

11. It is no good just saying that one does not ask
'Is it true?' in reading a poem though one does ask it in
reading a newspaper report. Doing what is not done is
being unconventional. It is not being stupid.

And it will not do to say that one cannot answer the
question for that only makes it seem like a hard question.
The question is unanswerable not in the way cancer is
incurable but in the way health is incurable. It is not a
hard question because it is not a question at all: It is a
confusion. It is just as much a confusion when asked on
reading Donne's line "Pleasure is none, if not diversifi'd"
as when asked on reading Eliot's line "O the moon shone
bright on Mrs. Porter."

12. I say to someone 'If you must read newspapers, the
only sensible way of reading them is with a skeptical eye.'
So as he reads I want him to ask himself every so often
'Is it true?.' That is a way of reading something. (Just so
a way, probably the only sensible way, of doing philosophy

is to keep asking oneself 'How do I know?' and if that leads to trouble then 'What do I mean?' and if that leads to trouble then 'How do I know?.') Asking oneself 'Is it true?' makes sense in reading newspapers, history books, and so on. I don't think it makes good sense in reading poetry.

There are different ways of reading different poems but none of them involve asking oneself 'Is it true?'. At least I do not think any of them involve asking oneself that sort of question. But I cannot prove it. There are too many different ways of reading poetry.

13. The heavens rejoyce in motion, why should I
Abjure my so much lov'd variety,
And not with many youth and love divide?
Pleasure is none, if not diversifi'd:

That is what Donne said. Is it true?

In philosophy *verum* but *in vino veritas:* there is truth in poetry as in wine and in much the same way. I say to a man 'There is some truth in Donne's *Elegie*.' He then goes through the lines looking for a true statement. And if I were to say '*In vino veritas,*' he would empty a bottle of wine waiting for the truth to drip out.

If you say 'It is true' of Donne's *Elegie* then the 'it' in 'It is true' is like the 'it' in 'It is raining.' For what is true? 'The poem is true' would be odd if said of the *Elegie*, and 'That is true' would be irrelevant if said of any of its lines in isolation and out of context. So not 'It is true' but 'There is (some) truth in it.'

For though to erre, be worst, to try truths forth,
Is far more businesse, then this world is worth.

VI

About 'God'*

MY text is a text—the utterance 'God exists.' The question is: does he?

1. The English utterance 'God exists' occurs in religious discourses in English (not in "religious language"—there is no such thing). The expression 'God' in that utterance is evidently a noun; furthermore, it is not a count noun (like 'bean') since it does not require an article. This is not to deny that there is also a count noun 'god' in English. Thus one can say 'If God exists then a god exists' or even 'God is a god.' This indicates that 'God' is not a noun like 'man' in 'Man is a rope stretched over an abyss' for one cannot say 'Man is a man.'

That 'God' is neither a pronoun nor a mass noun in the utterance 'God exists' is indicated by the fact that it is neither a pronoun nor a mass noun in English religious discourses; that it is neither a pronoun nor a mass noun in these discourses is indicated by various facts; that it does not occur in such environments as 'How much . . . exists?' 'A quantity of . . . exists'; that it takes 'he' as an anaphoric substitute as in 'That God exists may be doubted but that some men think he exists, that cannot

* Originally published in *Religious Experience and Truth*, ed. Sidney Hook (New York, 1961); reprinted by permission.

be doubted'; that the "wh—" form employed in connection with 'God' is generally 'who'; and so forth.

Hence it is reasonably clear that 'God' in 'God exists' is a proper noun, a proper name, or for short, a name.

2. A name may be introduced into a particular discourse either by both extralinguistic and intralinguistic means or simply by intralinguistic means. Since I take it that no one claims to have learned to use the name 'God' by extralinguistic means, no one (that I am concerned with) claims to have had the referent of the name 'God' indicated to him by ostension, we may take it that the name 'God' has been introduced into those religious discourses in which it occurs solely by intralinguistic means.

'God' then is a name like 'Caesar' or 'Pegasus' but not like your name.

3. To introduce a name into a discourse by intralinguistic means alone it is necessary to associate certain expressions of the discourse with the name. Since these expressions will have certain conditions associated with them, this means that derivatively the name will have certain conditions associated with it.

(To state the matter more clearly but less precisely, what I am saying is probably that which is intended by those who claim that certain names are introduced into a discourse by means of descriptions.)

4. Consider the name 'Dietrich of Leipzig': I tell you that Dietrich wrote theological tracts entitled "On the Divine Pseudonyms" and "Celestial Conundrums." I tell you that he lived in Leipzig about 1400.

I have now introduced the name 'Dietrich of Leipzig' into the present discourse. I have done so by associating with it certain expressions and, thus, derivatively a certain set of conditions. Thus the referent of the name 'Dietrich of Leipzig,' if it has one, is that which satisfied a certain set of conditions, a set having as its members the conditions of being a man, a resident of Leipzig about 1400, the author of certain theological tracts, and so forth.

5. I shall say that, speaking in what I take to be a familiar and relatively unproblematic way, the set of conditions we take to be associated with a name determines our conception of the referent of the name. Thus, given that the name 'Dietrich of Leipzig' has been introduced into the present discourse, you now have a certain conception of Dietrich.

6. Though a name may at one time have associated with it a certain set of conditions, at another time it may have associated with it a slightly different or even radically different set of conditions. If so, one's conception of the referent of the name will most likely have altered.

Thus your present conception of Dietrich may tarnish and alter in time. You may discover that he did not write the tract on pseudonyms; if so, you will then have a slightly different conception of Dietrich. Or you may discover that he did not write the tract on celestial conundrums, but rather a tract on infernal paradoxes, and indeed that he did not live in Leipzig about 1400. If so, you will then have a radically different conception of Dietrich.

A name is a fixed point in a turning world. But as the world turns, our conception of that which is named by a name may change.

7. The questions whether the name 'Dietrich of Leipzig' has a referent, whether Dietrich ever existed, whether any such person as Dietrich ever existed, or whether anything answering to our conception of Dietrich ever existed can all be answered in much the same way.

It is necessary to specify the relevant set of conditions associated with the name and then determine whether anything or anyone ever satisfied the conditions of the set.

8. Questions whether the name 'God' has a referent, whether God exists, whether any such being as God exists,

or whether anything answering to our conception of God exists can all be answered in much the same way and in much the same way as the analogous questions about Dietrich.

It is necessary to specify the relevant set of conditions associated with the name and then determine whether anything or anyone satisfies the conditions of the set.

9. But whether God exists is, in fact, a genuine question depends on (at least) two distinct factors: first, on the intelligibility of the conditions associated with the name, and secondly, on the consistency of that set of conditions.

To determine whether the conditions are intelligible and, if so, both self-consistent and mutually consistent, it is necessary to determine precisely what they are.

10. The first problem then is to specify the conditions associated with the name 'God.' And it is here that the confusion endemic in religious discourse takes its locus. We need not confuse the excubant theologian's febrile concept with that of a plain or even plainer man.

Different theistic groups are likely to have somewhat different and even competing conceptions of God. Presumably the God of the Christians is identical with the God of the Jews: yet Christians apparently suppose that the referent of the name 'God' satisfies the condition of either having been crucified or having had a crucified son; while Jews apparently suppose that the referent of the name 'God' satisfies the condition of neither having been crucified nor having had a crucified son. (It follows that either Jews or Christians are laboring under a misconception.)

Within a particular theistic group, the members of the group are likely to have different conceptions of God. And even a particular member of a theistic group is likely to have different conceptions of God at different periods of his life. To simplify matters I shall suppose that for the moment we are largely concerned with some particular conception of God.

11. All sorts of conditions have been associated with the name 'God.' For the purposes of the present discussion it is useful to sort some of these conditions into two groups, unproblematic conditions and problematic conditions.

12. Some unproblematic conditions are the conditions of being a being, a force, a person, a father, a son, a creator, spatiotemporal, crucified, just, good, merciful, powerful, wise, and so forth.

I class these conditions as unproblematic because it seems clear to me that each condition is, in fact, satisfied or readily satisfiable by something or someone; furthermore, that each condition is satisfied or readily satisfiable is a fairly obvious matter.

13. Some problematic conditions are the conditions of being omnipotent, omniscient, eternal, creator of the world, a non-spatiotemporal being, a spirit, the cause of itself, and so forth.

I class these conditions as problematic simply for this reason: If someone were to maintain that a traditional conception of God is unintelligible, I should think he would base his claim on the prior claim that such conditions as these are fundamentally unintelligible.

So the question is: Are such conditions as these somehow unintelligible?

14. To suppose that the conditions in question are unintelligible is to suppose that one cannot understand them. But understanding admits of degrees—I think there can be no doubt but that some of us at any rate have some understanding of these conditions.

I know that if something satisfies the condition of being an omnipotent being then there is nothing that it cannot do owing to a lack of power; such a being could transport a stone from the earth to the sun in less than one second. I know that if something is the cause of itself then we cannot succeed in finding another cause. I know that if something is the creator of the world then prior to its act of creation the world did not exist. And so forth. That I can make such inferences indicates that I have some understanding of the conditions involved.

15. The only general sort of reason I can think of to suppose that the conditions in question are somehow unintelligible is that it is evidently difficult to establish whether or not any of them are, in fact, satisfied. But although this is something of a reason to suppose that the conditions in question are somehow unintelligible, I do not think it is a good reason.

Understanding a condition is one thing; knowing how to establish that it is satisfied is another. For example, suppose I agree to do something on the condition that my friend George approves of it. There is no difficulty in understanding this condition though there may be some difficulty in establishing that it is satisfied. Suppose that I agree to do it on the condition that Caesar would have approved of it—there is still no difficulty in understanding the condition though there could be considerable difficulty in establishing that it is satisfied. And now suppose that I agree to do it on the condition that the last man ever to live, were he alive now, would approve of it: there is still no difficulty in understanding the condition and yet I have no idea how actually to establish that such a condition is satisfied.

16. I do not wish to deny that what I have called "problematic" conditions associated with the name 'God' pose all sorts of conceptual problems, including problems of verification and confirmation. Thus, is there a difference between the condition of being a spirit and that of being spirits? If so, how do we count spirits? What principle of individuation is employed? (This is, of course, an old

question, but all these questions are old questions.) Again, what is one to understand by creation *ex nihilo?* Of course, as Collingwood pointed out, one does not create something out of anything; thus we speak of creating a disturbance, a design. Even so, creation takes place in a certain environment, under certain environing conditions. The conception of first nothing and then something is a difficult one.

But despite such problems as these I do not think that there can be any serious question about the intelligibility of the conditions in question. That they pose problems merely shows, if it shows anything, that the conception of God is a difficult one.

17. Similarly, I am inclined to suppose that there can be no great problems about the self-consistency and mutual consistency of the conditions in question. Again, there are problems of a sort. I would not deny it; how can something satisfy both the condition of being a being and that of being nonspatiotemporal? I suppose numbers might be said to be nonspatiotemporal, but then numbers are not beings. Such problems, however, are readily dealt with in obvious ways: contradiction can always be avoided by an appropriate and judicious feat of logistic legerdemain; conditions can always be weakened, modified, and so made compatible. This game has been played for over a thousand years.

18. Consequently it seems reasonable to suppose that whether God exists is an intelligible question. To answer it we need do nothing more than determine whether the conditions associated with the name 'God' are satisfied. Since that is evidently difficult to do, the interesting question then is: why is it difficult and can it be done, now or ever?

19. The difficulty in establishing whether or not God exists is obviously partially attributable to the character of what I called the "problematic" conditions associated with the name 'God.' All such conditions seem to involve

99

some extreme form of either generalization or abstraction.

Thus the condition of being omniscient is an obvious generalization over the condition of being informed or learned. The condition of being the creator of the world can be thought of as a generalization over the condition of being a creator. On the other hand, the condition of being a nonspatiotemporal being can be viewed as the result of an abtraction from the condition of being a spatiotemporal being. The ease of such abstraction is testified to by the fact that plain people sometimes say they find it difficult to keep body and soul together.

20. The question we are concerned with is whether a certain set of conditions, conditions involving simultaneous generalization and abstraction, are satisfied. Questions of such a character are, I believe, not unreasonably classed as theoretic questions. Simultaneous generalization and abstraction is frequently a striking characteristic of scientific laws and hypotheses; thus a scientist may speak of all rigid bodies, of all bodies free of impressed forces, and so forth.

That a certain question is reasonably classed as a theoretic question is of interest only in that it indicates that one can reasonably expect to answer such a question only within the framework provided by a theory of some sort.

21. It is or should be evident that the question whether God exists can be answered only within the framework provided by some theory if it can be answered at all. For it is or should be obvious that no simple set of observations unsupplemented by powerful theoretic considerations can serve to determine whether or not anything satisfies the conditions in question, that of being an omnipotent being. That a certain being did not perform a certain task could not in itself establish that the being was not omnipotent, no matter what the task was. Again, that the being performed the task would not establish its omnipotence, and again that no matter what the task was. Projection or extrapolation of some sort is required but that is possible only within a theoretical framework.

22. But the difficulty in providing a final answer to the question whether God exists is only partially owing to problems posed by what I have called "problematic" conditions. It is primarily owing to the fact that, in fact, there is not one but indefinitely many questions to answer. That each question is asked by the utterance 'Does God exist?' only shows that we put old names to new uses. The sense of the question 'Does God exist?' depends on the conditions associated with the name 'God': these may vary from case to case and they change in time.

23. Consider a plain man's conception of God: the name 'God' has associated with it the conditions of being an omnipotent being, creator of the world, and so forth. Then in answer to the question 'Does God exist?' one can say this: There is no reason to suppose so; there is excellent reason to suppose that no such being exists.

It is a tenet of present physical theory that no physical object can attain a velocity greater than the speed of light. Consequently, according to present physical theory, no being has it in its power to transport a stone from the earth to the sun in one second. But this is to say that no omnipotent being exists. Hence, according to present physical theory, nothing answering to the plain man's conception of God exists.

Present physical theory may be mistaken; that is always possible. But that possibility is irrelevant here. For no matter what form physical theory may take in the future, it seems reasonable to suppose that it will impose certain limits on experience: the existence of limits is incompatible with the existence of an omnipotent being.

24. Present physical theory, however, does not suffice to establish the nonexistence of God; at best, it suffices to establish the nonexistence of God as now conceived of by a plain man.

Man's conception of the world he lives in changes; that his conception of a creator of the world also changes is only to be expected. In consequence the question 'Does God exist?' may be freshly conceived, and so conceived may call for a fresh answer. That the answers to the old questions have always been no proves nothing. The answer to tomorrow's question is something that one can only be blank about.

VII

On Understanding
Understanding Utterances *

1. OF course understanding an utterance is something complicated. I would not claim to understand exactly what is involved. But I want to suggest and explore at least one aspect of a certain way of understanding the understanding of utterances, a way having at least the virtue of leading us with ease along an edge of conjecture from perplexity to doubt. In this way we shall know what we do not know.[1]

2. Certain utterances can be understood without attending to the particular linguistic environment, i.e. the particular discourse, in which they occur or without attending to the context of utterance.

I say to you here and now: 'Hippopotami are graceful.' Possibly you have never before heard a person say this. Even so, you can and most likely do understand it. But if you do, it cannot be on the basis of the discourse in which the utterance has just occurred or on the basis of the context of utterance.

* Originally published in J. A. Fodor and J. J. Katz, *The Structure of Language*, © 1964; reprinted by permission of Prentice–Hall, Inc., Englewood Cliffs, N.J.

[1] I have here profited from various discussions with L. Gleitman, Z. Harris, H. Herzberger, and H. Hiz.

Even though not all utterances can be understood without attending to the particular discourse in which they occur or without attending to the context of utterance, there are nonetheless an indeterminate number of utterances that can be so understood. I propose to consider and examine closely at least part of what is involved in understanding such utterances before attending to the complications that arise in attending to the discourse and the context of utterance.

3. If I attribute an understanding of an utterance to you, what is it that I am attributing?

I shall suppose that the semantic analysis of an utterance consists in associating with it some set of conditions, that the semantic analysis of a morphological element having meaning in the language consists in associating with it some set of conditions, and I shall suppose this without further discussion here.[2]

Given such suppositions, it then seems reasonable to suppose this: that part of what is involved in understanding an utterance is understanding what conditions are relevantly associated with the utterance. Of course, this can only be part of what is involved in understanding an utterance. It is all that I shall be concerned with here.

4. Someone says 'Hippopotami are graceful' and we understand what is said. In some cases we understand what is said without attending to the discourse the utterance has occurred in or without attending to the context of utterance. How do we do it?

It seems reasonable to suppose that part of what is involved is this: Such an utterance is understood on the basis of its syntactic structure and morphemic constitution.

---

[2] See Paul Ziff, *Semantic Analysis*. Although these suppositions are ultimately of considerable importance in the analysis I shall present, they are of little importance within the confines of the present discussion. Anyone who objects to them may ignore them so far as the present discussion is concerned.

Assuming that part of what is involved in understanding an utterance is understanding what conditions are relevantly associated with the utterance, this means that we take a certain set of conditions to be associated with such an utterance on the basis of its syntactic structure and morphemic constitution.

5. But if this is so then understanding an utterance must somehow involve an apprehension of the specific syntactic structure of the utterance as well as an identification of its morphemic constitution.

I propose to say nothing here about morphological matters and hence nothing about the problems that arise in the identification of the morphemic constitution of an utterance. Instead, I shall be concerned with certain problems that arise in the apprehension of the syntactic structure of an ordered sequence of morphemes constituting an utterance.

6. The utterances of a natural language constitute an indeterminate set. Each member of the set has a syntactic structure. But although many utterances have the same structure, there are indeterminately many utterances of different structures.

Thus 'The cat that ate the rat is here' differs in structure from 'The cat that ate the rat that ate the cat is here' which in turn differs in structure from 'The cat that ate the rat that ate the cat that ate the rat is here' and so on.

7. If one understands an utterance then one has somehow apprehended the syntactic structure of that utterance. Since one can understand an indeterminate number of structurally distinct utterances this means that one can somehow apprehend an indeterminate number of distinct syntactic structures of an indeterminate number of utterances.

For this to be possible it is essential that the structure of the language be essentially projective in character. The apprehension of an indeterminate number of distinct syntactic structures of an indeterminate number of utterances must involve some sort of projection from some determinate finite basis. The utterances of the language must have a certain order and must be interrelated in certain ways. Apprehending the syntactic structure of an utterance is essentially a matter of locating that utterance in the structure of the language.

8. For theoretic purposes, the utterances of a natural language may be thought of as constituting an infinite set. Generally speaking, syntactic theory is in part concerned with the projection of an infinite set from some finite set on the basis of various procedures. But however this may be done, the projected infinite set will at best be an infinitely large proper subset of the infinite set of utterances of the language.

(An analogy may be helpful here: it is only an analogy. The well-formed formulas of a logistic system, of some familiar type, constitute an infinite set. Theorems of the system will constitute an infinitely large subset of the set of well-formed formulas. This infinitely large subset may be a projection from some finite set of axioms on the basis of certain procedures. But in the normal case the projected infinite set will at best be a proper subset of the infinite set of well-formed formulas: in the normal case, not every well-formed formula will be a theorem.)

9. Generally speaking, if one is concerned with semantic analysis it is useful to consider and, as it were, to operate with a proper subset of the set of what are traditionally classed grammatical utterances, the set of syntactically non-deviant utterances. For example, 'He stepped on a green thought' may be classed a grammatical utterance but, even so, it is syntactically deviant: one can readily discern a syntactic regularity in English which the utterance in question deviates from; the deviation is owing to the co-occurrence of 'green' and 'thought' in the given linguistic environment. Syntactically deviant utterances of English thus include

both those utterances exemplifying problems of co-occurrence as well as those utterances traditionally classed as ungrammatical.

The syntactically nondeviant utterances of a language are those utterances included in the finite set constituting the simplest and most adequate basis for projection as well as those utterances included in the projected infinite set. In consequence, the grammatical utterances of a language are primarily those utterances that accord simply with the dominant syntactic regularities to be found in the language.

(In terms of the preceding analogy, nondeviant utterances are analogous to theorems and not simply to well-formed formulas of a logistic system. That one can also think of the well-formed formulas of a logistic system as the analogues of nondeviant utterances in a natural language is here irrelevant: one analogy need not preclude another. And there is an important disanalogy here: for unlike theorems and nontheorems of a logistic system, no sharp line divides nondeviant from deviant utterances.)

10. To class an utterance of the language as syntactically deviant is not to claim that it is devoid of syntactic structure. If an utterance were devoid of syntactic structure it could not reasonably be classed as an utterance of any language whatever. Neither is it to claim that it is devoid of any syntactic structure peculiar to the language in question, for if that were the case the utterance could not reasonably be classed as an utterance of that language.

A syntactically deviant utterance of English is both an utterance of English and a deviant utterance in virtue of its structure. The utterance is an utterance of English in that its structure is that of an English utterance. But in so far as the utterance is syntactically deviant, its structure must differ from that of a nondeviant English utterance. Consider the utterances 'Man shoots woman' and 'The men grief the women': some of us can understand these utterances. That means that some of us can somehow apprehend the syntactic structures of these utterances. But these utterances are syntactically deviant, indeed ungrammatical in a traditional sense. And that means that the distinction between the nondeviant and the deviant cannot be a distinction between utterances having and utterances lacking structure: it can only be a distinction between types of structure.

11. Understanding an utterance involves an apprehension of the syntactic structure of the utterance, and apprehending the syntactic structure of an utterance is a matter of locating the utterance in the structure of the language.

Since the syntactically nondeviant utterances occupy a different position in the structure of the language from the syntactically deviant utterances, there is necessarily a difference between what is involved in understanding a syntactically nondeviant utterance and what is involved in understanding a syntactically deviant utterance. (And if one is to understand how it is that we do understand deviant utterances, it is essential to realize this.)

12. Apprehending the syntactic structure of a nondeviant utterance is a matter of grasping the simplest relation between the utterance and the set of nondeviant utterances.

Since the utterance in question is itself a nondeviant utterance and hence included in the set of nondeviant utterances, the simplicity of the relation between the utterance and the set of nondeviant utterances is essentially a matter of the internal simplicity of the set of nondeviant utterances. And since the set of nondeviant utterances is an infinite set projected from some finite basis, the simplicity of the set is a matter of the simplicity of the finite basis and of the procedures of projection.

13. Apprehending the syntactic structure of a syntactically deviant utterance is also a matter of grasping the simplest relation between the utterance and the set of nondeviant utterances. But since the utterance in question is not itself a nondeviant utterance, the simplicity of the re-

lation between the utterance and the set of nondeviant utterances is not a matter of the internal simplicity of the set of nondeviant utterances.

A deviant utterance has that structure that constitutes the terminus of the simplest route from the regular grammar to the utterance in question.

14. The concept of the simplest route from the regular grammar is I believe essential to the understanding of understanding deviant utterances. But to explicate precisely what such a concept involves and to illustrate its fruitfulness it is necessary to consider, if only briefly, the structure of the set of nondeviant utterances.

The structure of a set of nondeviant utterances is described by a grammar of the language. A grammar is a syntactic system of elements corresponding in certain specifiable ways to elements of the language in question. The syntactic system (not described but only suggested here) will be that developed by Noam Chomsky.[3]

15. Syntactically nondeviant utterances are both those utterances, called "kernels," included in the finite set constituting the simplest basis for projection as well as those utterances, called "transforms," that are included in the projected infinite set.

The class of kernels is some finite class of structured n-tuples of morphological elements of the language. More particularly, the kernels of a language are those utterances of the language having the simplest structure and providing the most adequate basis for projection. Thus presumably utterances like 'The house is red,' 'The cat is on the mat,' 'The man eats the cake' would be kernels of English.

16. A particular kernel structure may be defined by a set of rules in a syntactic system, a grammar. The rules of the grammar correspond (more or less) to the dominant regularities to be found in the language.

For example, the structure of 'The man eats the cake'

[3] See *Syntactic Structures*.

or of 'The woman eats the pie' can be defined by the following set of rules: (where → is read "can be rewritten as," and where S is the class of sentences, NP is the class of noun phrases, VP is the class of verb phrases, T the class of definite articles, V the class of verbs, and N the class of nouns)

1. $S \rightarrow NP_1\text{-}VP$
2. $NP_i \rightarrow T\text{-}N_i$
3. $VP \rightarrow V\text{-}NP_2$

and the utterance 'The man eats the cake.' may then be derived by adding the following rules:

4. $T \rightarrow$ 'the'
5. $N_1 \rightarrow$ 'man,' 'woman'
6. $N_2 \rightarrow$ 'cake,' 'pie'
7. $V \rightarrow$ 'eats'

(Rules 1–7 are offered here merely by way of example, not as actual rules of English grammar.)

17. The class of transforms is an infinite class of structured n-tuples of morphological elements of the language. The structure of a transform may be thought of as the result of a complex operation over structures of one or more kernels.

The structure of a particular transform may be defined by a set of rules in the grammar. For example, the structure of 'The cake was eaten by the man' can be defined in the grammar by adding to the previous set of rules the optional rules:

8. $NP_1\text{-}V\text{-}NP_2 \rightarrow NP_2\text{-}be\text{-}V\text{-}en\text{-}by\text{-}NP_1$
9. $be\text{-}$'eats'$\text{-}en\text{-}by \rightarrow$ 'is eaten by'

(Of course, in an actual grammar one would not introduce an isolated and limited rule like 9. Instead, one would formulate more general morphophonemic rules and rules pertaining to tenses of which the effect of 9 would be a consequence.) The structure of the transform 'The cake is eaten.' can then be defined by adding the further optional rule:

10. $NP_2\text{--}be\text{--}V\text{--}en\text{--}by\text{--}NP_1 \rightarrow NP_2\text{--}be\text{--}V\text{--}en$

18. Whether or not an adequate grammar of English will contain rules 1–10, or rules like them, depends primarily on two factors: first, on whether such a grammar enables us to derive a set of sentences conforming to our intuitive notions of what constitutes the set of grammatical utterances; secondly, on the simplicity of the syntactic system. For example, instead of 8 one could adopt the rule:

8'. $T\text{--}N_1\text{--}V\text{--}T\text{--}N_2 \rightarrow T\text{--}N_2\text{--}be\text{--}V\text{--}en\text{--}by\text{--}T\text{--}N_1$

and instead of 10 one could adopt the rule: (where $\emptyset$ indicates deletion)

10'. $by\text{--}Np \rightarrow \emptyset$

Whether 8 or 8' or 10 or 10' should be adopted can be decided on the grounds of the adequacy and the simplicity of the resultant syntactic system.

19. Consider such utterances as: 'House the is red,' 'I saw man kiss woman,' 'The men the women kiss,' 'The men grief the women,' 'Over there is a green thought,' and 'He expressed a green thought.'

Intuitively speaking, one is inclined to say different things about these different utterances, while at the same time saying that all are deviant. 'House the is red' sounds simply like a mistake, or possibly a childish way of talking. But 'I saw man kiss woman' sounds like something a foreigner would say: one can almost hear a foreign voice uttering it. 'The men the women kiss' sounds like a bit of poetry, while 'The men grief the women' has the air of a semi-clever remark. One is inclined to say that 'thought' in 'Over there is a green thought' has a nonliteral use, whereas not 'thought' but 'green' has a nonliteral use in 'He expressed a green thought.'

All such intuitions can be explicated in terms of the concept of the simplest route from the regular grammar.

20. Consider the utterance 'He expressed a green thought': it might seem as though the utterance were deviant owing simply to the combination of 'green' and 'thought.' That this is not the basic reason is indicated by the fact that the class of elements that can occur without syntactic deviation in the environment 'He expressed a green . . .' is null, thus 'He expressed a green tree' is also deviant. Hence the deviance of 'He expressed a green thought' cannot be attributed to 'thought.' It can only be attributed to 'green.' Let E_i be the class of elements that can occur without syntactic deviation in the environment 'He expressed a . . . thought': then we can relate the utterance to the regular grammar by invoking the rule $E_i \rightarrow$ 'green.'

On the other hand, the utterance 'Over there is a green thought' is deviant owing to the occurrence of 'thought.' Let E_j (where $i \neq j$) be the class of elements that can occur in the environment 'Over there is a green. . . .': then by invoking the rule $E_j \rightarrow$ 'thought' we can relate the utterance to the regular grammar.

Since the deviance of 'That is a green thought' can be attributed either to 'green' or to 'thought,' apart from a particular discourse or context of utterance, the utterance is ambiguous: one could be referring either to a green thing or to a certain thought.

21. The utterance 'The men the women kiss' has a poetic sound to it. It is also ambiguous for one can easily hear it as equivalent to 'The men kiss the women' or to 'The women kiss the men.' That it is deviant is owing to the fact that it has the form $NP_i\text{-}NP_j\text{-}V$: presumably no such structure can be derived as the structure of a single sentence in the regular grammar. Thus 'The men the women kiss' should not be confused with the nominalized utterance in 'The men the women kiss are here,' for this utterance is

related to the kernels 'The men are here' and 'The women kiss the men.'

One could relate the utterance 'The men the women kiss' to the regular grammar by invoking either the rule $NP_i\text{–}V\text{–}NP_j \to NP_i\text{–}NP_j\text{–}V$ or the rule $NP_i\text{–}V\text{–}NP_j \to NP_j\text{–}NP_i\text{–}V$. In so far as either route from the regular grammar is equally simple, the utterance must be structurally ambiguous. Note that if one were concerned with the utterance 'The man the cake ate' only the rule $NP_i\text{–}V\text{–}NP_j \to NP_i\text{–}NP_j\text{–}V$ would do; if one were instead to invoke the rule $NP_i\text{–}V\text{–}NP_j \to NP_j\text{–}NP_i\text{–}V$, one could derive 'The man the cake ate' only if 'The cake ate the man' were a nondeviant utterance: presumably no such utterance can be derived in our regular grammar.

That the utterance 'The men the women kiss' has a poetic sound is simply owing to the fact that inversions corresponding to the invoked rules occur primarily in poetic discourses. In such discourses such structures serve a useful purpose for they are productive of ambiguities.

22. The utterances 'The men grief the women,' 'I saw man kiss woman,' and 'House the is red' offer no difficulties here.

The first requires the rule $E_k \to$ 'grief', where E_k is the class of elements that enter into the transformation 'The men caused the women E_k' $\to$ 'The men E_k the women,' e.g. 'The men caused the women trouble' transforms to 'The men trouble the women.' The second calls for a rule having the effect of $Ar \to \emptyset$, where Ar is the class of articles. Utterances that are deviant owing to the deletion of articles are frequently encountered in news reports and in the speech of foreigners. Notice that an utterance like 'I saw men kiss women' may simply be the plural counterpart of the ungrammatical 'I saw man kiss woman,' in which case it too is deviant—and in such a case one can hear the accent of a foreigner. The third, 'House the is red' sounds simply like a mistake owing to the fact that it obviously calls for the rule $T–N \to N–T$ and such a rule would (generally) be utterly pointless.

23. Various problems are posed by this method of analysis. But the most obvious and pressing are these: How does one find a route from the regular grammar to the utterance, and what determines which of alternative routes is the simplest?

24. How one finds a route from the regular grammar to the utterance is primarily a matter of identifying the source of the utterance's deviance. Having done that it is no great problem to invent and invoke the rule to suit the purpose. But identifying the source of deviance can be an exceedingly subtle and difficult task. The problem can, however, be divided.

There are (at least) two prominent types of deviation that can be distinguished. Certain utterances deviate in regular ways, others in irregular ways.

What I am suggesting is this: that the utterances of a language can be divided into at least four relatively distinct syntactic classes (distinct perhaps as red, blue, green, and yellow are distinct): the class of kernels, the class of transforms, the class of what I shall call "variants," and the class of what I shall call "inventions."

25. Variants are utterances that deviate from the syntactic regularities of the language in some regular way. Thus they are variations on standard themes.

Whether a deviant utterance is a variant is indicated by the type of rule that must be invoked to relate it to the regular grammar in the simplest possible way. With respect to variants the simplest type of rules involve either inversion or deletion or addition. Thus 'The man the cake ate' is an instance of inversion; 'Man eats woman in lifeboat' is an instance of deletion; 'The a man a that a I a saw a is a here a' is an instance of addition.

26. Inventions are utterances that deviate from the syntactic regularities of the language in irregular ways. Thus

they are not variations but, as it were, genuine inventions.

Whether a deviant utterance is an invention is also indicated by the type of rule that must be invoked to relate it in the simplest possible way to the regular grammar. With respect to inventions the simplest type of rules involve either the extension of word classes or the contraction of word classes. Thus 'The men grief the women' is an instance of invention calling for the extension of a word class. Contraction, however, is a more complicated matter.

27. Cases involving the contraction of word classes warrant special mention here for they occur only when there is some sort of semantic difficulty; thus they are not strictly syntactic in character though they have a syntactic effect.

Consider the utterance 'Even though my heart is in my chest and I am in the lowlands, my heart is in the highlands': unless we distinguish between the two occurrences of 'heart' or among the three occurrences of 'in' we have a self-contradictory utterance. The simplest way to resolve the difficulty is to assume that a contraction of a word class is involved.

Let E_o be the class of elements to which the environment 'My . . . is in the highlands' is open. We then invoke a rule to the effect that 'heart' is a member of E_o on the prior supposition that it is not; this may be written as

$$-(E_o \rightarrow \text{'heart'}) \mid E_o \rightarrow \text{'heart'}$$

where the expression to the left of the vertical line indicates that the rule expressed by the expression to the right of the vertical line is invoked on the supposition expressed by the expression to the left of the vertical line. The effect of the supposition is to make the utterance 'Even though my heart is in my chest and I am in the lowlands, my heart is in the highlands' deviant. Then by invoking the rule we relate the utterance to the regular grammar. If this procedure seems unduly artificial, it should be noted that the supposition was dictated by our desire to avoid a semantic difficulty, whereas the rule was invoked merely to relate the utterance to the regular grammar.

Another type of word class contraction is exemplified by 'Josef is a boy but George is a child': again, the simplest way to avoid a semantic difficulty is to assume that a contraction of a word class is involved. Let E_c be the class of elements to which the environment 'George is a . . .' is open. We then invoke the rule to the effect that 'child' is a member of E_c on the prior supposition that 'boy' is not: thus:

$$-(E_c \rightarrow \text{'boy'}) \mid E_c \rightarrow \text{'child'}$$

Still another type of word class contraction is exemplified by 'A dog is a dog but a cat is a cat.' Generally speaking, word class contraction always involves a prior supposition that a certain class is closed to a certain element and the invocation of a rule to the effect that a certain class, perhaps another class, is open to a certain element, perhaps another element.[4]

28. What I should now like to suggest is this: that there are five basic types of routes from the regular grammar to a syntactically deviant utterance. In consequence, there are five types of rules that may be invoked; (where capital letters are variables for word classes and lower case letters are variables for words) these five types of rules may be rendered schematically as follows:

1. . . . A . . . B . . . $\rightarrow$ . . . B . . . A . . .
2. . . . A . . . B . . . $\rightarrow$ . . . A . . .
3. . . . A . . . $\rightarrow$ . . . A . . . B . . .
4. $A \rightarrow a$
5. $-(A \rightarrow a) \mid B \rightarrow b$

[4] I am inclined to suppose that word class contraction is intimately related to so-called "appreciative" and "depreciative pregnancies" in the use of words. See William Empson, *The Structure of Complex Words*.

The first is the rule of inversion, the second of deletion, the third of addition, the fourth of word class extension, and the fifth of word class contraction.

(It should be noted that rules of the form $a \rightarrow b$, e.g. 'the' → 'house,' have been excluded from consideration here. For example, an utterance like 'I put the door out and closed the cat' is perhaps best dealt with by invoking the pair of rules 'door' → 'cat' and 'cat' → 'door.' But this is a matter of morpheme identification. Intuitively speaking, one draws a line between say 'House the is red,' a case of inversion, and 'I put the door out and closed the cat,' a case of morpheme identification. How the line is drawn is a complex matter that I cannot discuss at this point.)

I am inclined to suppose that these five basic types of rules constitute the simplest type of routes from the regular grammar to syntactically deviant utterance types.

29. Answering one question here always seems to give rise to another: what reason is there to suppose that the simplest routes are the five indicated? That I feel inclined to say so proves nothing; that you agree with me, if you do, still proves nothing.

The five types of rules indicated do not of course exhaust the list of possible rules. For example, one could formulate a mad rule like $ABCDEFG \rightarrow CBAEGDF$. Given such a rule one could then directly relate an utterance like 'Saw man the the it window in.' to the regular grammar.[5] Indeed, it would be a variant of 'The man saw it in the window.' So by designating the five indicated types of rules as the

---

[5] Note that on the simplest analysis 'Saw man the the it window in.' would be a semi-grammatical utterance, for it could be a transform by deletion: thus according to the rules $NP_i\text{-}V\text{-}NP_j \rightarrow NP_j$, $NP \rightarrow N\text{-}N\text{-}N\text{-}N\text{-}N\text{-}N\text{-}N$, it would have the form ' 'Saw,' 'man,' 'the,' 'the,' 'it,' 'window,' 'in.' ' As such, the utterance might occur as a response to 'What are the words?' or 'What did you say?' and so forth. Further note that this interpretation would be consistent with the natural intonation contour of such an utterance, viz. a contour indicative of a list.

simplest routes, an infinite number of others have been excluded. But with what justification?

Here I am inclined to say this: that the five types of rules indicated somehow reflect the basic structure of the language, for they seem to follow what at present seems to be the general pattern of transformations. Thus inversion occurs in the passive and in interrogative transformations, addition in conjunctive transformations, deletion in all sorts of transformations, while word class extension is a feature of nominalizing transformations.

30. However, even if I am right in claiming that these five types of rules constitute the simplest types of routes back to the regular grammar, so far I have at best characterized, as it were, the logical space of operations. There is still the problem of deciding in a given case which of alternative routes is the simplest; one could relate the utterance 'The men grief the women' to the regular grammar by invoking either the rule $E_k \rightarrow$ 'grief,' where E_k is the class of elements that enter into the transformation 'The men cause the women E_k' $\rightarrow$ 'The men E_k the women,' or the rule $E_m \rightarrow$ 'grief,' where E_m is the class of elements that can occur without deviation in the environment 'The men . . . the women,' or the rule $V \rightarrow$ 'grief,' where V is the class of verbs.

No doubt the simplicity of a route must depend on the strength of the rule, the character of the classes involved, and so forth. But I can say nothing helpful about these matters here.

Finally, I have so far said nothing about the significance of syntactically nondeviant utterances. If we relate a deviant utterance to the regular grammar by invoking certain rules, how do the rules serve to determine the significance of the utterance? To answer this question we must first consider how the structure of a nondeviant utterance serves to determine the significance of the utterance. That is a long and difficult story.

VIII

About Ungrammaticalness[*]

IS the sentence 'He had a green thought' ungrammatical?
Some say "Of course not" and at once, without hesitation.
I say:

1. Grammatical theory is a complex subject, abounding
in technicalities. I mean to avoid technicalities here in so
far as I can. The points I want to make are, to begin with
anyway, fundamentally simple. They can be understood
without a detailed investigation of their divers ramifica-
tions. So I shall for the most part speak in a relatively
vague and intuitive way, using plain words even in cases
where more technical locutions are available and would be
vastly more precise. I shall also take various things for
granted.

2. I know and I shall take for granted that 'He had a
green thought' is an English sentence. Thus one can
sensibly ask whether or not it is a grammatical English
sentence. (How I know that that is an English sentence
is a hard question. The identification of an expression as
a particular English sentence involves phonetic, phonemic,
morphological, syntactic, and nonsyntactic semantic considerations. I do not want to go into the question here but,
as will be seen, I cannot altogether avoid it.)

[*] Originally published in Mind, LXXIII (1964); reprinted by
permission.

3. Suppose we have a grammar of English. Then, speaking somewhat vaguely, we could ask whether or not the sentence 'He had a green thought' is in accordance with the grammar. (What the phrase 'in accordance with the grammar' is supposed to mean is far from clear, how it is understood will depend on what kind of grammar is being considered.) Suppose the sentence is in accordance with the grammar. Then if the grammar is a correct grammar of English, we should have to say that the sentence 'He had a green thought' is a grammatical English sentence.

So the important question is: Is the grammar a correct grammar of English?

4. I think the point I am making here is obvious. But since some seem inclined to deny it, I mean to labor it a bit.

Some seem to think that since they were not taught at school not to say 'He had a green thought,' there's nothing ungrammatical about the sentence. The sentence is grammatical according to the grammar they learned at school, so the sentence is grammatical.

The obvious reply to this is the point I'm laboring, that if the grammar they learned at school is a correct grammar of English then what they say is so. But is the grammar they learned at school a correct grammar of English?

"The way I speak is in accordance with the grammar I learned at school": but is it?

5. To know whether a grammar is a correct grammar of English we have to have some idea whether or not various expressions are grammatical English sentences and we have to determine whether or not these sentences are in accordance with the grammar.

This can be said in another way. Before we can hope to assess the correctness of a grammar, we have to have some intuitive idea of grammaticalness. An adequate grammar will be one that captures this intuition (and perhaps does other things as well). (A choice between alternative grammars might be based on considerations of simplicity, utility in teaching the language to foreigners, and so forth.) So let us look at the matter in an intuitive way.

6. Intuitively and somewhat vaguely speaking then, a native speaker balks when an ungrammatical sentence is uttered (other than by way of example, quotation, and the like and apart from rather special and specifiable contexts and discourses). (A more precise technical term is available here. Instead of speaking of speakers balking when a sentence is uttered, we could speak of semantically deviant utterances and semantically deviant sentences.[1] Thus a sophisticated reader of poetry does not balk at the phrase 'a green thought' in Marvell's *The Garden*; even so, it is semantically deviant.) Thus if children speak ungrammatically, some of us are apt to correct them; some of us take steps to get them to cease talking in that way.

This suggests one necessary condition of ungrammaticalness, that if a sentence is ungrammatical then native speakers balk when the sentence is uttered. (The qualification "unless the sentence is uttered by way of quotation, example, and the like and apart from rather special and specifiable contexts and discourses" is of course required, but I shall not bother to say all this each time it may be necessary. My aim in this paper is to convey some intuitive understanding of ungrammaticalness, that and nothing more.)

7. Consider the sentence 'He don't believe it': is this sentence ungrammatical?

I say yes and no, for it depends on which dialect of English the sentence is supposed to occur in. In certain dialects of American English, such a sentence is grammatical: native speakers do not balk when it is uttered. (Indeed, in some cases such speakers might look askance at the sentence 'He doesn't believe it.') In other dialects

[1] See Ziff, *Semantic Analysis*, for an explication of the concept of a semantically deviant utterance.

of English, speakers do balk when the sentence 'He don't believe it' is uttered. In such cases the sentence can perhaps be correctly classed as ungrammatical. (I do not deny that some people believe that 'He don't believe it' is ungrammatical even when native speakers do not and are not apt to balk at the sentence. There is no accounting for what some people believe.)

8. Suppose I say 'It's raining' when it is not raining. Then what I've said is not so. A native speaker of English aware of the state of the weather might balk when I utter the sentence 'It's raining': after all, if children go around saying things that are not so, some of us take steps to get them to cease. So why not class the sentences uttered in saying what is not so as ungrammatical?

One reason is this: I might say 'It's raining' when it is raining. There need be nothing to balk at in such a case.

9. If I say 'It's raining' when it is not raining, a native speaker might balk at what I say but he would not be apt to balk at the sentence. Even if he did balk at the sentence, he would be balking at the sentence token, not the sentence type.

It is not necessary to confuse sentence tokens and sentence types. 'That's a cow' and 'That's a cow' are two different sentence tokens of one sentence type.

A sentence is ungrammatical if and only if every token of the sentence type is ungrammatical. Ungrammaticalness pertains primarily to sentence types.

Thus if I utter the sentence 'It's raining' when it is not raining and we class this sentence token as ungrammatical then we must also class the token 'It's raining,' uttered when it is raining, as ungrammatical. And this means that we would be balking at tokens that we have no reason to balk at.

10. But this is also something that wants explaining: Why does ungrammaticalness pertain primarily to sentence types and not sentence tokens?

Suppose we were to class only certain sentence tokens

of a certain sentence type as ungrammatical. It would follow that it would not be possible to tell whether or not a given sentence token of the type in question was ungrammatical simply by examining the token. For since it is only by virtue of what they have in common that two sentence tokens are tokens of the same type, there could be no relevant difference between them on the basis of which one but not the other could be correctly classed as ungrammatical. (But this is not to deny that there are homonymous sentence types. For example, in the spoken language, 'I saw an Alaskan bare' and 'I saw an Alaskan bear' are homonymous sentence types. Again, the ungrammatical sentence 'I were going to the store' need not be identified with the homonymous expression that occurs in the sentence 'If I were going to the store, I would get it for you.' The latter expression may well be a morphophonemic variant of the grammatical sentence type 'I was going to the store.')

11. So, still intuitively and somewhat vaguely speaking, I suppose we can say this: If a sentence is ungrammatical then native speakers balk when an arbitrary token of the type is uttered. But there is more to be said.

If a sentence is ungrammatical, not only do native speakers balk when the sentence is uttered but they balk at it in that they balk because of certain structural features of an arbitrary token of the type.

For example, in certain dialects of English, the sentence 'He don't believe it' is ungrammatical. Not only do the speakers of these dialects balk when such a sentence is uttered but their basis for doing so is quite clear. Thus grammatically sophisticated and articulate speakers of such dialects would point out that the subject pronoun 'he' calls for the third person singular form 'does' instead of 'do' (or 'doesn't' instead of 'don't').

12. It is time to be a bit more precise, and unfortunately, a bit more technical.

A grammar of a language can be thought of as a system

of some sort (though it can also and perhaps profitably be likened to a machine, or a device, or a procedure) for attributing structural descriptions to certain expressions of the language. Thus if we had a correct grammar of English, it would be possible correctly to attribute a structural description to any English sentence or expression whatsoever, whether grammatical or not. (If we could not do that, we could have no reason for classing a given expression either as an English expression or as an English sentence.)

Furthermore, the set of structural descriptions attributable to certain expressions of the language will, in a correct grammar of the language, be divided into at least two exclusive proper subsets. I shall speak of the set of accepted structural descriptions and of the set of nonaccepted structural descriptions. Supposing we have a correct grammar of the language, I shall say that a sentence of the language is grammatical if and only if its associated structural description is a member of the set of accepted structural descriptions. I shall say that a sentence of the language is ungrammatical if and only if its associated structural description is a member of the set of nonaccepted structural descriptions.

13. If a sentence is ungrammatical then, in a correct grammar of the language, that sentence will have a nonaccepted structural description. And this means that the sentence will have a structural description that is classed as nonaccepted on theoretic grounds. (If it were not so classed on theoretic grounds, it could not be so classed in the grammar.)

So suppose we say this: A sentence of a language is ungrammatical if and only if first, native speakers of the language balk when an arbitrary token of the type is uttered, and secondly the sentence type has an associated structural description that is classed as nonaccepted on theoretic grounds.

And the question now is: What must a structural description be like if it is to be classed as nonaccepted on theoretic grounds?

14. Given a correct grammar of a language, an ordered set of categories can be associated with a given sentence. The categories in question may be word categories, *Noun, Adjective, Verb*, or word-group categories, *Noun-phrase Verb-phrase, Subject, Predicate, Sentence, Passive Sentence.* (In more sophisticated grammars, the categories may be construction types, or constituent types, or transformational types, and so forth. To avoid unnecessary complications and technicalities, I shall here be concerned simply with word and word-group categories.)

To give a structural description of a sentence is to associate an ordered set of categories with the sentence. (Thus in a familiar phrase-grammar, the ordered set {*Sentence, Noun-Phrase, Verb-Phrase, Definite Article, Noun, Verb, Adjective*} constitutes a structural description of the sentence 'The cat is hungry.')

15. For a structural description to be classed as non-accepted on theoretic grounds, it must be possible to designate an ordered set of categories as nonaccepted. But if this were all there was to it, then any structural description whatever could be classed as nonaccepted on theoretic grounds. Thus any given sentence type that occasions a balk by native speakers could then be classed as ungrammatical.

For example, knowledgeable native speakers might conceivably balk when the sentence 'An oyster isn't a bivalve' is uttered, though presumably they would not balk when the sentence 'An oyster is a bivalve' is uttered. Let us introduce and invoke the categories C_1 and C_2 such that 'an oyster' falls under C_1 and 'isn't a bivalve' falls under C_2. We can then designate the ordered set of categories {C_1, C_2} as nonaccepted.

The obvious objection here is that the categories that have been introduced and invoked are completely *ad hoc.* (That we would also have introduced an asymmetry here by classing only the negative form of a sentence as ungrammatical is a relevant but not a conclusive point. At a relatively casual level of analysis, such asymmetry is already to be found in the language; 'I haven't any money' is grammatical but 'I have any money' is ungrammatical, and so is 'It's not the case that I have any money.' However, there is good reason to say that 'I haven't any money' is the negative form not of 'I have any money' but rather of 'I have some money.' Given such a transformational analysis one could perhaps deny that such asymmetry is in fact already to be found in the language.)

16. When are categories *ad hoc* and when not? That is an enormously difficult problem that I must and mean to side-step for the time being. (But see below.) Let us suppose that somehow we can assign a degree of utility to a category or to an ordered set of categories such that the degree of utility will be the inverse of the degree of *ad hocness*.

Presumably even in a correct grammar of a language the grammatical categories will differ in degree of utility. Thus intuitively speaking, I suppose that the category *Noun-Phrase* is of greater utility than the category *Mass Noun*. (Any measure of utility would, I believe, have to accord with such an intuition to be acceptable.) But presumably in anything that we are prepared to call a correct grammar of a language, all the categories will be of a sufficient degree of utility to avoid the charge of *ad hocness*. (For if the categories were not of such a degree of utility, the systematic character of the grammar would be called into question.)

17. Let n be the minimum degree of utility sufficient to avoid the charge of *ad hocness*. Then, supposing again that we have a correct grammar of the language, we can say that a sentence of the language has a degree of ungrammaticalness greater than zero if and only if its associated structural description is in terms of an ordered set of categories such

that the ordered set is of a degree of utility equal to or greater than n and where the structural description is a member of the class of nonaccepted structural descriptions.

Intuitively speaking, I am inclined to suppose that the degree to which a native speaker is apt to balk when an ungrammatical sentence is uttered could (in part anyway) be accounted for in terms of the degree of ungrammaticalness of the sentence. For example, a native speaker of my dialect is likely to balk when the sentence 'I have a elephant' is uttered, but such a speaker would balk more strongly when the sentence 'I has an elephant' is uttered. This difference probably reflects the difference in the degree of ungrammaticalness. The sentence 'I have a elephant' exemplifies a deviation with respect to a morphophonemic category: before a vowel, the sandhi form 'an' is required. Presumably such a category is of only minor utility. But the sentence 'I has an elephant' exemplifies a deviation with respect to a proper subcategory of the category *Verb*, the subcategory in question being of considerable utility, or so I am inclined to suppose.

(But it must be understood that these remarks are of a speculative and intuitive character. In default of a measure of utility, one cannot speak otherwise.)

18. Is the sentence 'He had a green thought' ungrammatical? Do native speakers of the relevant dialects balk when the sentence is uttered (other than by way of example, quotation, and the like and apart from rather special and specifiable contexts and discourses, for example, in poetry)? I think they do. (Whether a speaker is apt to balk of course depends not only on the utterance but on the speaker. But such complications are easily avoided if one proceeds in a more precise but more technical way, by considering whether or not the utterance in question is semantically deviant. An intuitive account of complex matters can be achieved only at the cost of vagueness and imprecision.)

At least one distinguished philosopher maintains that 'He had a green thought' is grammatical but nonsensical. To say that what is said in saying 'He had a green thought' is nonsensical is to balk when the sentence is uttered, at least in the loose sense of 'to balk when the sentence is uttered' that I intend here.

Of course, in so far as the philosopher insists that the sentence is grammatical, it might seem that he cannot be said to balk at the sentence. He does not think he's balking at the sentence uttered, he thinks he is balking at what is said in uttering the sentence. But maybe he is confused about what he is balking at. And anyway, it is clear enough that he balks when the sentence is uttered, and that is all that is required here. (I shall not discuss whether or not 'He had a green thought' is nonsensical. However, I can see not the slightest reason to suppose that it is nonsensical. When Andrew Marvell wrote "Annihilating all that's made to a green thought in a green shade" he was not making a mistake, neither did he write anything nonsensical.)

19. The question then is: Does the sentence 'He had a green thought' have a structural description that can be classed as nonaccepted on theoretic grounds?

Can we attribute to the sentence a structural description belonging to the class of nonaccepted structural descriptions, where the structural description is in terms of categories of a sufficiently high degree of utility to avoid the charge of *ad hocness*? To determine this, we have to determine which categories are relevant, and then we must in some way assess the degree of utility of the ordered set of categories associated with the sentence.

It is, I believe, quite clear that if we restricted our attention to categories presumably of a relatively high degree, to *Noun, Verb, Adjective*, the sentence 'He had a green thought' would have to be classed as grammatical. More simply, in so far as we are concerned with categories of such a degree, there is nothing exceptional to be noted in connection with the phrase 'a green thought': it is simply an example of a noun phrase, not differing in that respect from 'a green house' or 'a pink flower.'

Hence if the question is whether 'He had a green thought' is ungrammatical at some extremely high level of ungrammaticalness, the answer would seem to be no. It does not follow that it is not ungrammatical to some lesser degree.

20. Consider such sentences as 'The fool is utter,' 'The fool is out and out,' 'She hurt himself.' Are these sentences ungrammatical? It would be hard to deny it.

But it is, I believe, quite clear that if we restricted our attention to categories presumably of a relatively high degree of utility, to *Noun, Verb, Adjective,* these sentences would have to be classed as grammatical. More simply, in so far as we are concerned with such categories, there is nothing exceptional to be noted in connection with the expression 'is utter': it is simply an example of a verb phrase, not differing in that respect from 'is tall' or 'is morose.'

A somewhat subtler analysis is evidently called for.

21. Consider the sentence 'It's nice to have tree': is this sentence ungrammatical? I am inclined to suppose so. But if it is, what is ungrammatical about it?

The word 'chicken' in English falls under the category *Count Noun* and also under the category *Mass Noun,* and thus under the disjunctive category *Count/Mass Noun,* all of which are proper subcategories of the category *Noun.* The relevant difference between mass nouns and count nouns is that the former requires neither an article nor a plural affix. Thus the sentence 'It's nice to have chicken' and the sentences 'It's nice to have a chicken' and 'It's nice to have chickens' are all grammatical. But if 'tree' is simply a count noun and not a mass noun, and if these categories have a degree of utility equal to or greater than n, the sentence 'It's nice to have tree' is ungrammatical.

To avoid sentences that, intuitively speaking, are clearly

ungrammatical, it is necessary to attend to categories presumably of a lesser degree of utility than those of *Noun, Verb, Adjective*. In particular, we must introduce and invoke proper subcategories of these categories.

22. We must introduce and invoke proper subcategories of the familiar categories cited. But how many?

I suggest: a great many, about 7,023. (Why that number? It is a nice big number and a big number is what is wanted here.) If a grammar is, as it were, to capture the intuition of even ordinary speakers and hearers, a great variety of categories is called for.

It will help here to look at the matter in a general way.

23. One might suppose that ideally every sentence type that occasions a balk should be classed as ungrammatical. Such an ideal (whether desirable or not) is unattainable. Alternatively, one might suppose that every sentence type that is itself balked at (and not merely one that occasions a balk) should be classed as ungrammatical. But even this ideal is in fact unattainable.

There are limits to what a grammar can enable us to do while still retaining its character as a grammar.

24. Is 'She hurt himself' ungrammatical? I am inclined to say so. Just so. 'The lady hurt himself,' 'The woman hurt himself,' 'His wife hurt himself,' etc. are all ungrammatical in my dialect of English.

Suppose we introduce a category of feminine and a category of masculine expressions: thus 'wife,' 'woman,' 'herself,' etc. are feminine expressions; any endocentric noun construction with a feminine expression as head is also a feminine expression: thus 'the lady in the hallway' is a feminine expression. The category of masculine expressions could be specified in the same way. We could then designate the structural description associated with 'She hurt himself' as nonaccepted owing to the fact that the environment 'hurt —— + self' is open only to expressions of the same category with respect to masculine or feminine. (The details of such an analysis are somewhat complex, but the point is simple enough.) So we could say that 'She hurt himself' and 'His wife hurt himself' are ungrammatical.

25. But now consider the sentences 'His wife hurt himself' and 'The adult female person he is married to hurt himself.' These sentences may not be exactly synonymous but the difference in significance is surely slight. Even so, we can hardly maintain that 'The adult female person he is married to hurt himself' is ungrammatical, and this despite the fact that native speakers would be apt not only to balk when the sentence is uttered but to balk at the sentence. To class such a sentence as ungrammatical, very special categories would have to be introduced and invoked. Presumably such categories would be of little utility. And perhaps more significantly, the same sort of difficulty would only crop up again.

For consider the sentence 'The person of the opposite sex he was married to before he became a man hurt herself': this sentence poses the same problem. To avoid it, we should have to maintain that the expression 'the person of the opposite sex he was married to before he became a man' falls under the category *Masculine*. But on what grounds, or more precisely, on what syntactic grounds? Or to make matters even worse, consider the environment 'The person of the sex opposite to his at that time since when he has changed sex seven times, that person hurt —— + self': what fills the blank, 'him' or 'her'? Assuming that elementary arithmetic is not a part of grammar, this is not a grammatical question.

26. There are limits to what a grammar can enable us to do while still retaining its character as a grammar. But the exploration of these limits and the determination of precisely what does and what does not fall within these limits is a subtle and difficult task for grammarians. This

is not an area in which the idle pronouncements of philosophers are apt to be illuminating.

Are the following sentences ungrammatical?

> He wants my own hat.
> A perfect fool is looked by him.
> I have any books.
> A filth is to be avoided.
> Puppies look barking.
> The fork eats.
> He was reading bore books.
> The men grief the women.
> He has a red good apple.
> He had a green thought.

In each case, to answer the question calls for work. To say anything sensible here, one has to leave the prim path of rosy speculation and muck about with the data. I shall illustrate this (if only briefly) in connection with 'He had a green thought.'

27. Let us introduce and invoke the categories N_s and A_s such that 'thought,' 'fact,' 'idea,' 'statement,' 'proposition' fall under the word category N_s, and such that 'interesting,' 'strange,' 'surprising,' 'true,' 'possible,' etc. but not 'green' fall under the word category A_s. (Thus the categories in question can be effectively characterized by a complete list of the words that fall under them.) Let $-A_s$ be the category of words that do not fall under the category A_s. We can then designate the ordered set of categories {Article, $-A_s$, N_s} as a member of the set of nonaccepted structural descriptions. Thus 'He had a green thought' is ungrammatical.

28. The question now is: Are the categories in question, N_s, A_s, and $-A_s$ of a sufficient degree of utility to avoid the charge of *ad hocness*? In default of any measure of

utility, no precise answer can be given to this question. Even so, we can look at the matter in an intuitive way.

29. Consider the following pairs of sentences:

(1a) He had a green thought.
(1b) He had a strange thought.
(2a) The thought that George was alive was green.
(2b) The thought that George was alive was strange.
(3a) That George was alive was green.
(3b) That George was alive was strange.
(4a) It was green that George was alive.
(4b) It was strange that George was alive.

Notice that when 'green' is replaced by 'strange' there is nothing strange. Further notice that the members of N_s are all intimately associated with sentences; technically speaking they appear to be sentence nominalizations, they replace sentences. The members of A_s are also intimately associated with sentences; technically speaking they appear to be sentence adjuncts, they occur as modifiers of sentences.

I suggest that this is very strong evidence and thus a very strong indication that the categories introduced and invoked are not wholly *ad hoc*. (Technically speaking, sentences (1b-4b) indicate that the categories in question will be of utility in a transformational analysis of English.)

Is 'He had a green thought' ungrammatical? That depends on what the or a correct grammar of English proves to be. But for the time being I am certainly inclined to suppose that it is.

IX

About What an Adequate
Grammar Could Not Do *

THERE is much that an adequate grammar of a natural language could not do, open an oyster, for example, but then, who would have thought it could? The pearls some hope to be disclosed by a grammar are of a rarer sort: insight into the structure of the language, an understanding of the linguistic capacities and behavior of the native speakers, and so forth.

But along with its undoubted incapacity to open an oyster there is something else that an adequate grammar could not do which many do seem to suppose that it could, namely discriminate between ambiguous and unambiguous sentences. That it could not is what I shall try to show.

1. What an adequate grammar of a natural language could or could not do depends on what an adequate grammar is or would be. A grammar of course, but when would it be adequate? Of this large question only a small part need be considered here.

There are various conditions of adequacy that one could seek to impose on a grammar with respect to ambiguity. So one might say: (I) if a sentence is ambiguous then the

* Originally published in *Foundations of Language*, I (1965).

grammar should provide more than one syntactic structural description for the sentence; or (II) the grammar should provide more than one syntactic structural description for a sentence only if the sentence is ambiguous; or (III) the grammar should provide more than one syntactic structural description for a sentence if and only if the sentence is ambiguous.

Conditions (I), (II), and (III) do not exhaust the possibilities. I mean to reject all three as unreasonable and offer in their place quite another. But for the moment there are other matters.

2. I would not suggest that anyone has suggested that condition (III) or condition (I) would be a reasonable condition to impose on a grammar with respect to ambiguity. It is conceivable that someone has but I do not know that.

Condition (II) has in fact been offered by Noam Chomsky. Thus, where "f is a function such that $f(i,j)$ is the set of structural descriptions of the sentence s_i that are provided by the grammar G_j," Chomsky says that "$f(i,j)$ should contain more than one structural description only if the sentence s_i is ambiguous—that is, this is a reasonable empirical condition, one of many, on the grammar of a language".[1]

3. If any of the conditions mentioned were acceptable as reasonable conditions on the adequacy of a grammar, my claim that an adequate grammar could not discriminate between ambiguous and unambiguous sentences would be either wholly or partially in error.

If condition (III) were fulfilled by a grammar, one could simply identify the set of ambiguous sentences of the language with the set of sentences having more than one structural description. The grammatical discrimination between ambiguous and unambiguous sentences would thus be complete. If condition (I) and not (II) were fulfilled, the set of ambiguous sentences would be a proper subset of

[1] "On the Notion 'Rule of Grammar,'" *Structure of Language and Its Mathematical Aspects*, pp. 6–7.

the set of sentences having more than one syntactic structural description. Although this would not enable one to establish grammatically that a given sentence is ambiguous, it would in some cases enable one to establish grammatically that the sentence is not ambiguous. Thus the grammar would make at least a partial discrimination between ambiguous and unambiguous sentences. Conversely, if condition (II) and not (I) were fulfilled, the set of sentences having more than one syntactic structural description would be a proper subset of the set of ambiguous sentences. And though this would not enable one to establish grammatically that a given sentence is not ambiguous, if condition (II) were fulfilled in a nontrivial way, it would in some cases enable one to establish grammatically that the sentence is ambiguous. Thus again the grammar would make at least a partial discrimination between ambiguous and unambiguous sentences. (But see Section 6 below.)

But in maintaining that an adequate grammar could not discriminate between ambiguous and unambiguous sentences, I mean to say that there is not a single sentence with respect to which such a grammar would enable one to establish grammatically either that it is or that it is not ambiguous.

4. Condition (I) is that if a sentence is ambiguous then the grammar should provide more than one syntactic structural description for the sentence. That this would constitute an absurd demand to make on a grammar is no doubt obvious. But it is not irrelevant to consider precisely why.

The reason is not that no grammar could meet the condition. On the contrary, one could because one could easily construct one of the requisite sort. For example, consider the remark 'I saw a shark': since the remark can be, the sentence is said to be, ambiguous. Am I referring to the denizen of a pool or a poolroom? But nothing precludes the possibility of our constructing a (silly) grammar in which the word 'shark' is assigned to two distinct noun categories with the result that in that grammar the sentence 'I saw a shark' could be assigned two distinct syntactic structural descriptions in terms of the distinct noun categories.

5. There are at least two reasons why condition (I), and in consequence condition (III), would constitute an unreasonable demand to make on a grammar.

The first is that even though a grammar could fulfill condition (I), it could do so only at an extreme cost. A grammar could provide two distinct syntactic structural descriptions for a sentence like 'I saw a shark,' but doing so would necessitate invoking an incredible number of wholly *ad hoc* categories, categories that would be of virtually no utility and would hardly figure elsewhere in the grammar.[2] Such a grammar would thus perversely gain in arbitrariness what it lost in simplicity.

The second reason why condition (I), and in consequence condition (III), would constitute an unreasonable demand to make on a grammar will be explained later in connection with a difficulty with condition (II).

6. Condition (II) is that the grammar should provide more than one syntactic structural description for a sentence only if the sentence is ambiguous. There are two cases to be considered for there are two different ways in which a grammar could fulfill this condition.

First, it could do so trivially simply by not providing more than one syntactic structural description for any sentence of the language. Secondly, the grammar could fulfill the condition in a nontrivial way, thus it would provide more than one syntactic structural description for some sentences of the language, each of which would in fact be ambiguous.

I shall consider the second case first, that in which a grammar fulfils the condition in a nontrivial way. It will not be difficult to see that the grammar will then inevitably be open to precisely the same objection already lodged

[2] See Chap. VIII above.

against a grammar fulfilling condition (I): it will at best be arbitrary and complex owing to its unavoidable reliance on wholly *ad hoc* means.

7. What is wanted here to begin with are examples of ambiguities and these are plentiful.

If I say 'I saw the shooting of the hunters' am I saying that I saw the hunters shooting or that I saw the hunters being shot? (Other alternatives we can presently ignore.) Again, 'He was shot by his sister': did his sister shoot him or was he shot alongside his sister? Still again, 'The man tore up the street': was the street torn up by the man or was it up the street that he tore? And one may think of such expressions as 'a large oyster bed,' 'a small boys school,' 'a rusty red knife,' and so on.

8. It is and I shall later show that it is reasonable to expect that in an adequate grammar of English a sentence like 'I saw the shooting of the hunters' will be assigned (at least) two distinct syntactic structural descriptions. Assuming that the grammar fulfills condition (II) in a nontrivial way, we may assume that it provides (at least) two distinct syntactic structural descriptions for the sentence 'I saw the shooting of the hunter' and, in consequence, it may be inferred that the sentence is ambiguous. Since that sentence is ambiguous, all seems well, at least at first glance. But there are other cases to consider.

'I saw the shooting of the apes': is this sentence ambiguous? Did I see the apes being shot or the apes shooting? After all, apes might learn to handle firearms. So, yes, it is ambiguous. Intuitively speaking, it seems clear that the sentences 'I saw the shooting of the hunters' and 'I saw the shooting of the apes' have the same, or if not exactly the same then virtually the same, syntactic structure. Consequently if in the grammar one is, then both must be, assigned double syntactic structural descriptions. Since both sentences are ambiguous, this does not seem to pose any problem with respect to the fulfillment of condition (II).

But now what shall we say about the sentence 'I saw the shooting of the elephants'?

9. If we stare at the following pairs of sentences we can see a difficulty staring out at us:

> I saw the shooting of the children.
> I saw the shooting of the elephants.

> He was shot by the ape.
> He was shot by the elephant.

> The man tore up the street.
> The man tore up the ticket.

> I found a large oyster bed.
> I found a succulent oyster bed.

> They are visiting railroad men.
> They are visiting railroad stations.

The first member of a pair is ambiguous, the second is not. Yet, intuitively speaking, each pair exemplifies the same or virtually the same syntactic structure.

If a grammar is to fulfill condition (II) in a nontrivial way it must provide more than one syntactic structural description for some sentences of the language but only those that are ambiguous. But this means that the grammar must assign different syntactic structures to some such pairs of sentences as those here listed. For it does not matter what example one takes: a mere morphological change can always suffice to eliminate the ambiguity supposedly being exemplified and supposedly attributable to the syntactic structure of the sentence.

10. Could a grammar fulfill condition (II) in a nontrivial way? Perhaps conceivably it could, but if it could, it could do so only by employing wholly *ad hoc* categories.

To consider but a single case, since the environment 'I saw the shooting of the . . .' yields an ambiguous sentence when the blank is filled by 'hunters,' 'men,' 'children,' 'apes,' 'monkeys,' but not when the blank is filled by 'elephants,' 'sows,' 'eggs,' 'meat,' one could arbitrarily invoke two special categories in terms of which one could hope to preclude the assignment of double syntactic structural descriptions in one case and not the other. But even this heroic measure would not suffice: there are further problems to cope with.

A word like 'hunters' would presumably have to be assigned to both categories in as much as the word can be used to refer either to persons or to horses and horses cannot shoot. In any case it would be necessary to distinguish between the ambiguous 'I saw the shooting of the iron shod hunters' and the unambiguous 'I saw the shooting of the split hooved hunters,' between the ambiguous 'I saw the shooting of the shouting hunters' and the unambiguous 'I saw the shooting of the whinnying hunters,' and so on.

I believe we may safely conclude without further discussion that a grammar that fulfilled condition (II) in a nontrivial way would inevitably be sufficiently arbitrary and complex to warrant being disqualified as an adequate grammar of the language.

11. Suppose then a grammar fulfilled condition (II) trivially simply by not providing more than one syntactic structural description for any sentence of the language: could such a grammar qualify as an adequate grammar of the (English) language? The answer to this question can be found in connection with the second reason why conditions (I) and (III) must be rejected as constituting unreasonable demands on a grammar.

There are many ways of thinking about and viewing a grammar of a language, but it can hardly be denied that a grammar is directly and immediately primarily concerned with word arrangements, with sequences of words, with relations between words and words. A grammar is not, or not directly and immediately, primarily concerned with relations between words and nonlinguistic things.

The sentence 'I saw a shark' is ambiguous. But the ambiguity does not arise from and is not either directly or indirectly owing to the particular arrangement of the words in the sentence. Thus it would be unreasonable to suppose that the arrangement contributes to the ambiguity. This can be seen in the fact that, with a little but not over much stretching of the imagination, innumerable syntactically diverse sentences in which the word 'shark' is used can be or anyway can seem somewhat ambiguous.

So I believe we can say this: Since the ambiguity of sentences like 'I saw a shark' is not of a type that falls within the province of grammar, it would be unreasonable to expect an adequate grammar of the language to deal with such cases. And the question then is: When is the ambiguity of a sentence of a type that does fall within the province of grammar?

12. There is an answer to this question that can be stated in general terms or there is no answer at all.

We are here concerned to evaluate, and if possible to formulate, a condition on the adequacy of a grammar, a condition that can be appealed to in the evaluation of a grammar. This means that it is necessary to answer the question in general terms eschewing all references to the particular categories of a particular grammar. This can be done.

13. Since ambiguity is not an uncommon feature of discourse it is not surprising that means are available in discourse for the resolution of ambiguities. Typically one queries the ambiguous sentence by posing alternatives. Thus one might query 'I saw a shark' with 'Do you mean a man or a fish?'. But one can think of these alternatives as suggesting alternative rephrasals of the original sentence, and so one might ask 'Do you mean "I saw a man" or "I saw a

141

fish"?'. Just so, one might query the ambiguous (written) sentence 'I found a large oyster bed' with 'Does it mean "I found a large bed of oysters" or "I found a bed of large oysters"?'

But now consider the difference between the rephrasals of these two ambiguous sentences:

(1a) I saw a man.
(1b) I saw a fish.
(2a) I found a large bed of oysters.
(2b) I found a bed of large oysters.

The difference between (1a) and (1b) turns on and reduces to that between the words 'man' and 'fish'. It has nothing to do with the arrangement of words. But the difference between (2a) and (2b) is clearly a matter of the arrangement of words.

To take a more complex case, consider (3a) and (3b)

(3a) I saw the children shooting.
(3b) I saw the children being shot.

offered as rephrasals of 'I saw the shooting of the children.' Is the difference here a matter of the arrangement of words? The difference between (3a) and (3b) reduces to that between 'shooting' and 'being shot', thus it bears a superficial resemblance to that found between (1a) and (1b), the difference between 'man' and 'fish.' There are, however, semantic considerations that indicate that the resemblance is merely superficial, that the former difference is in fact indirectly a matter of the arrangement of words.

Sentences (3a) and (3b) may not be equivalent in truth value. Consequently the difference between them must be indicative of this possibility. Now consider (4) and (5):

(4) The children are shooting policemen.
(5) The children are being shot by policemen.

(4) and (5) clearly need not be equivalent in truth value just as (3a) and (3b) need not. The difference between

them reduces to that between 'shooting' and 'being shot by.' But now consider (6).

(6) Policemen are shooting the children.

Unlike (4) and (5), (6) and (5) are equivalent in truth value. Nonetheless the apparent difference between (6) and (5) is the same as that between (4) and (5), namely that between 'shooting' and 'being shot by.' To account for the equivalence of truth values in one case, the possible lack of it in the other, we should be forced to conclude, and rightly, that the difference between 'shooting' and 'being shot' is in fact indirectly a matter of the arrangement of words, for (6) and (4) differ only in that.

14. I am inclined to suppose that the ambiguity of a sentence can sensibly be said to be of a type that falls within the province of grammar if and only if an arrangement of words contributes either directly or indirectly to the presence of the ambiguity. I am also inclined to suppose that a reasonable condition on the adequacy of a grammar would then be this: if the ambiguity of a sentence is of a type that falls within the province of grammar then the grammar should provide more than one syntactic structural description for that sentence.

A grammar that fulfilled this condition would then provide more than one syntactic structural description for a sentence like 'I saw the shooting of the hunters.' And no doubt in consequence it would also provide more than one syntactic structural description for the sentence 'I saw the shooting of the elephants' or even for 'I saw the shooting of the eggs.' But only a misconception of the nature of ambiguity could lead one to suppose that this would be an undesirable consequence.

15. A remark like 'I see a shark' is likely to be ambiguous only in a most unlikely sort of context. But because it can be we are or may be inclined to say that the sentence, which one employs to make the remark, is ambiguous. I think

that what is important here is this: we say that a sentence-type is ambiguous if and only if there is or could be a semantically nondeviant token of the type that is ambiguous. And this means that it may be desirable on occasion to distinguish between two quite different bases for the attribution of ambiguity. For one may attribute ambiguity to a sentence-type on the basis of the ambiguity of a semantically nondeviant token of the type. Or one may attribute ambiguity to a sentence-token on the basis of its being a token of an ambiguous sentence-type.

Thus if while pointing to a grim grey fish off the bow I say 'I see a shark,' my remark is not likely to be ambiguous. The sentence-token I uttered was not ambiguous. However in so far as that token was a token of a type of which there is or could be a semantically nondeviant ambiguous token, there is a sense in which I could rightly be said to have said something ambiguous. Unless we take care here we may find ourselves saying that the sentence-token both is and is not ambiguous, which, though it may be true in a sense, is not necessarily the plainest way of putting things.

I shall say that a sentence-token is ambiguous if and only if in employing the token one is making an ambiguous remark, or comment, statement, observation, etc. I shall say that a sentence-type is ambiguous if and only if there is or could be a semantically nondeviant ambiguous token of the type. I shall say of any token of an ambiguous sentence-type (and of certain other tokens as well) that the token has a potential for ambiguity. Whether or not the potential is realized will of course depend on further factors. For example, even though 'I see a shark' conceivably is an ambiguous sentence-type, the token employed in the context previously indicated would hardly be ambiguous: owing to the character of the context, its potential for ambiguity could not be realized.

16. If we are to understand the linguistic source of ambiguity, we must attend to the source of a sentence's po-

tential for ambiguity. Both 'I saw the shark' and 'I saw the shooting of the children' are ambiguous sentence-types. Consequently tokens of the types have a potential for ambiguity. But when we consider the two sentence-types we see at once that the source of the potential is different: in the first case, the source is morphological, in the second, syntactic. I shall accordingly speak of a morphological potential and of a syntactic potential for ambiguity.

For the realization of a morphological potential for ambiguity an appropriate context is required. But for the realization of a syntactic potential, both an appropriate morphemic constitution and an appropriate context are required. A token of the type 'I saw the shooting of the children' is ambiguous only if the token occurs in an appropriate context. It can be ambiguous because given its morphemic constitution its syntactic potential for ambiguity can be realized. On the other hand, a semantically nondeviant token of the type 'I saw the shooting of the elephants' cannot be ambiguous. But the reason is simply that such a token's potential for ambiguity cannot be realized owing to the nature of its morphemic constitution. From the fact that a sentence-type is not ambiguous, it does not follow that either the type or its tokens cannot sensibly be said to have a syntactic potential for ambiguity.

17. To attribute a syntactic potential for ambiguity to a sentence-type and to tokens of a sentence-type of which no semantically nondeviant token is ambiguous is to employ a form of projection, to operate in a systematic way. But that is only to be expected if one is concerned with grammar.

There is nothing particularly perplexing about the form of projection required here. The sentence-type 'I saw the shooting of the children' is ambiguous. Upon analysis we find that tokens of the type have a syntactic potential for ambiguity. We conclude that tokens of any sentence-type having the same syntactic structure as this sentence also have a syntactic potential for ambiguity. That many such sentence-types are not in fact ambiguous can then be explained in terms of their morphemic constitutions which serve to preclude the occurrence of an ambiguity.

Conversely, one can then explain certain matters that would otherwise go unexplained. For example, one need not be baffled by one's understanding of the following sequence of sentences found in a fairy tale: 'Did you see the shooting of the elephants? Yes, the elephants were using elephant guns.' The explanation is obvious: owing to the fact that the relevant sentence-token occurring in the fairy tale is semantically deviant, the restrictions imposed by the morphemic constitution of the sentence-type are overcome allowing the realization of the sentence's syntactic potential for ambiguity.

18. Could an adequate grammar discriminate between ambiguous and unambiguous sentences? Of course not.

If a grammar is to be an adequate grammar of the language then it should provide more than one structural description for all ambiguous sentences (types of course) whose ambiguity is of a type that falls within the province of grammar. Furthermore, the grammar cannot be largely arbitrary and arbitrarily complex. But any grammar meeting these requirements will inevitably fail to discriminate between ambiguous and unambiguous sentences.

That 'I saw the shooting of the apes' is, while 'I saw the shooting of the elephants' is not, ambiguous is not a grammatical fact. No sensible grammar could discriminate between such sentences. All that one can sensibly ask of a grammar is that it provide a means of discriminating between those sentences that do and those that do not have a syntactic potential for ambiguity.

That elephant guns are used on but not by elephants is an unfortunate fact, but the pain it causes a grammarian need be no greater than that of any other humanitarian.

146

X

The Nonsynonymy of Active
and Passive Sentences*

THAT a sentence in the passive is synonymous with its correlative active is a common misconception. It feeds on a failure to grasp and appreciate differences between questions of reference and those of meaning.[1]

1. The contrary is not uncommonly claimed: thus J. J. Katz and P. M. Postal, compounding confusion, have recently stated that "both actives and passives containing quantifiers and pronouns are ambiguous in the same way and so are full paraphrases of each other." [2]

This implausible pronouncement can be examined on the following rack of cases:

(1a) Everyone pleases his wife.
(1b) His wife is pleased by everyone.
(2a) No one is liked by his wife.
(2b) His wife likes no one.

* Originally published in *The Philosophical Review*, LXXV (1966); reprinted by permission.
[1] Research for this article was done while serving as a consultant for the Information Retrieval Staff of System Development Corporation, Santa Monica, California.
[2] *An Integrated Theory of Linguistic Descriptions*, p. 72.

(3a) Just a few people attended each wedding.
(3b) Each wedding was attended by just a few people.
(4a) Only the fresh meat was tasted by every tiger.
(4b) Every tiger tasted only the fresh meat.

That the (a)s are ambiguous is reasonably clear. That the (b)s are not equally so is equally clear. (With respect to (1a), is a certain lady in question or is it each one's own wife?; the same for (2a); for (3a), is it the same or a different small group at each wedding?; for (4a), is it that some but not every tiger tasted some stale meat or, though here one has, I think, to force it a bit, is it that only the fresh meat was tasted by tigers?) If one squirms, can one manage to read the (a)s and the (b)s alike? But then any distinction can be dulled in the light of a dim theory.

Less perspicuous counterexamples are also everywhere at hand: 'Everyone is frightened by his house' is ambiguous in a way that 'His house frightens everyone' is not, though this difference is not wholly a matter of quantifiers or pronouns: the former but not the latter admits of the interpretation that everyone is frightened either alongside a certain house or alongside his own house. Again, 'I saw some logs' is ambiguous in a way that 'Some logs were seen by me' is not, while the latter is again ambiguous in a way that the former is not. Alternatively, despite the syntactic and morphological similarity to (1a), 'Everything pleases his wife' is not equally ambiguous, and neither is 'Everyone murdered his wife.'

2. Certainly the above listed (b)s would seem more ambiguous if they were embedded in some appropriate context. Katz and Postal further claim that, if that is so, the (b)s must be genuinely ambiguous: they say that it is clear "that a particular constituent cannot have a given reading in a sentence context unless that reading is one of the constituent's readings in isolation." [3]

Thus on their flocculent theory 'pleasant' must, among

[3] *Ibid.*, p. 73.

many things, mean the same as 'unpleasant,' which conclusion is unpleasant. For if someone makes a harsh remark
and another, speaking in a dry tone, says 'That was a pleasant thing to say,' to read him right one must read 'unpleasant' for 'pleasant'; and since that would be reading
him right, that must be one of the readings of 'pleasant'
in isolation. Who would have thought it? And is one
reading of 'He refused to marry the young couple' this:
'He installed another fuse in order to fasten two lines
together'? For one could embed that sentence in a long
sentence as a conjunct in which to read it right, it must be
so read; for one could tell a long story about a robot turned
sailor and a young couple turned into rope by an Indian
rope dancer who was really an old fakir and so forth.

The claim that a particular constituent cannot have a
given reading in a sentence context unless that reading
is one of the constituent's readings in isolation is of course,
as it stands, absurd. To turn it true it is necessary to revise
the proviso to read: unless that reading either is or is a
derivative of one or more of the constituent's readings in
isolation. (Thus 'unpleasant' is not one of the readings of
'pleasant' in isolation, but it is a derivative of one of
those readings, the device of derivation being that of
irony, a relatively simple trope.)

That the listed (b)s would seem more ambiguous if
embedded in some appropriate context may be so, but
that would not suffice to establish that they are genuinely
ambiguous. For one would have to show that the contextual reading was not simply a derivative attributable to
the operation of contextual factors.

3. But it is not necessary to muddle up matters of
ambiguity with questions of synonymy. When ambiguities are at play, synonymy looks to be intransitive. For
example, (5):

(5) He refused.

is ambiguous in a way unlike either (6) or (7):

(6) He declined.

(7) He installed another fuse.

Even so, ignoring niceties: (5) and (6) are synonymous, (5) and (7) are synonymous, but (6) and (7) are not synonymous. If greater precision is wanted here, and it is, one can say that (6) is sentence-specific synonymous with (5), by way of indicating that a specific construal of (5) is in question. (Analogously, one can then speak of word-specific synonyms, phrase-specific expressions, sense-specific words, and so forth.) The ambiguity of sentences can then be characterized as follows: A sentence S_i is ambiguous if and only if there are sentences S_j and S_k (where $i \neq j \neq k$) such that S_j is sentence-specific synonymous with S_i, S_k is sentence-specific synonymous with S_i, S_j and S_k are not sentence-specific synonymous, and neither S_j nor S_k are semantically deviant.[4]

Consider (8a) and (8b):

(8a) No married man is liked by his wife.

(8b) His wife likes no married man.

Presumably (8a) is sentence-specific equivalent to (2a), 'No one is liked by his wife,' for if it is his own wife that is in question then the man must be married; but isn't it clear enough that (8b) is not sentence-specific equivalent to (2b), 'His wife likes no one'? But this is to say that (2a) and (2b) are not equally ambiguous.

Sentences (1a), (2a), etc. are ambiguous. Their correlative passives are not equally so. But even if they were, that fact would not suffice to establish that the passives are or are not sentence-specific synonymous with their actives.

4. Consider the following situation: There has been an altercation, someone struck someone, a single blow was

---

[4] The use of the word 'specific' was suggested to me by John Olney.

struck; George and Josef are the pair in conflict; there are various witnesses. The first reports (9):

(9) George struck Josef.

A second reports (10):

(10) George was struck by Josef.

These two reports are conflicting and so the sentences employed in making the reports would appear to be nonsynonymous. But this point needs careful sharpening if we are to pin down the right conclusion.

If two reports are in conflict, it does not follow that the sentences employed in making the reports are nonsynonymous. For example, suppose the first witness, pointing to George, had said (11):

(11) He struck the blow.

whereas the second, pointing to Josef, had said (12):

(12) He struck the blow.

Given the indicated characterization of the situation, these two reports are conflicting, yet it does not follow that sentences (11) and (12) are nonsynonymous.

If two reports conflict then there must be a difference somewhere which serves to account for the conflict. Here the conflict between reports (11) and (12) is readily accounted for in terms of the difference between the nonverbal behaviors of the witnesses: the first witness pointed to George, the second to Josef. Thus the conflict between reports (11) and (12) is owing to a difference in reference, not to a difference in meaning.

5. To return to our altercation, two other persons are present. These two do not know the name of either party involved. Thus the third witness says, pointing first to George and then to Josef, (13a):

(13a) That man struck that man.

But the fourth says, pointing first to George and then to Josef, (13b):

(13b) That man was struck by that man.

Note that there was no difference in the nonverbal behaviors of the third and fourth witnesses: both pointed first to George and then to Josef. Further note that reports (13a) and (13b) conflict. This conflict can readily be accounted for in terms of the nonsynonymy of (13a) and (13b). Yet (13b) would appear to be the passive correlated with (13a) and hence, on the thesis in question, the pair must be synonymous. So so much the worse for that thesis.

   6. Consider (14) and (15):

(14) A woman strikes a man.
(15) A woman is struck by a man.

These two are not synonymous: that they are not is not a fact unique, apart; it is a datum to be incorporated as an integral part of a coherent semantic theory. The nonsynonymy of (14) and (15) is readily aligned with the nonsynonymy of 'to strike' and 'to be struck'; this then is of course of a piece with the nonsynonymy of 'strikes a man' and 'is struck by a man,' from which it follows that to speak of striking a man is not the same as speaking of being struck by a man; thus that which is said of the woman referred to in (14) is not the same as that which is said of the woman referred to in (15). So it is reasonably clear that (14) and (15) cannot be synonymous.

   Given the nonsynonymy of (14) and (15), given that that which is said of the woman referred to in (14) is not the same as that which is said of the woman referred to in (15), how is one to avoid concluding that, like (14) and (15), (16a) and (16b)

(16a) A man strikes a man.
(16b) A man is struck by a man.

are nonsynonymous owing to the fact that that which is said of the person chiefly in question is different in each case?

And then what is there to say about such a pair as (17a) and (17b):

(17a) No one spoke to anyone.
(17b) No one was spoken to by anyone.

Are these too supposed to be synonymous?

7. Consider now such a simple pair as (18a) and (18b):

(18a) The tiger ate the man.
(18b) The man was eaten by the tiger.

Since to eat a man is hardly the same as to be eaten by a tiger, and since that which is said of the tiger in (18a) is hardly the same at that which is said of the man in (18b), what is it that makes some think that (18a) and (18b) might somehow, after all, be synonymous? Sadly enough, is it not only this: one is true if and only if the other is true? That such equivalence is insufficient to establish synonymy is an old story which by now should not need retelling.[5]

While excogitating the problems posed for such a thesis by tautologies and contradictions, a couple of cases should suffice; consider (19) and (20):

(19) Someone was a child.
(20) Someone was a parent.

Are these two synonymous? Yet one is true if and only if the other is. And again, shall we say that (21) and (22)

(21) Someone is a wife.

---

[5] But perhaps it does, e.g. see Chomsky, *Aspects of the Theory of Syntax*, p. 22, where to one's sorrow one finds the remark "The sentences (9i) and (9ii) are 'cognitively synonymous': one is true if and only if the other is true." But perhaps the quote marks around the dubious expression are intended to indicate just that.

(22) Someone is a husband.

are synonymous, for again one is true if and only if the other is?

8. In default of any plausible theory, much less a presumptive analysis, of sentence synonymy, it is difficult today to say much about the relation between the significance of a sentence like (18a), 'The tiger ate the man,' and the significance of a sentence like (18b), 'The man was eaten by the tiger,' a correlative passive. That they are somehow related in significance seems reasonably clear, for otherwise one would be hard put to explain the fact that though neither is either a tautology or a contradiction, one is true if and only if the other is true.

But that, though closely related in significance, they are nonsynonymous is also presently reasonably clear.

XI

*About Behaviorism**

"ONE behaviorist meeting another on the street said 'You feel fine! How do I feel?.'" This bad joke embodies two bad arguments against behaviorism. I want to explain why they are bad arguments.

1. I say 'I am angry.' My statement is true if and only if a certain organism is behaving in certain ways. If I say 'George is angry,' my statement is true if and only if a certain organism, viz. George, is behaving in certain ways. The only way I can tell whether or not George is angry is by observing George's behavior, verbal or otherwise. (There is nothing else to tell.) But I do not find out whether or not I am angry by observing my own behavior because I do not find out whether or not I am angry. (That I sometimes suddenly realize that I am or that I have become angry is essentially irrelevant here.) To talk of my finding out whether or not I am angry is generally odd: it would not be odd only in peculiar cases.

2. The first bad argument is not particularly interesting. It is this: If my being angry were a matter of my behaving in certain ways then I should be able to find out whether or not I am angry for I can find out whether or not I am

* Originally published in *Analysis*, XVIII (1958); reprinted by permission.

behaving in certain ways. Since it is generally odd to speak of my finding out whether or not I am angry, my being angry cannot be a matter of my behaving in certain ways. (Thus: "How do I feel?")

The mistake here is in the assumption that I can find out whether or not I am behaving in the relevant ways. A behaviorist maintains that to be angry is to behave in certain ways. I shall accordingly speak of 'anger behavior' and of 'anger behaving.'

It is generally odd to speak of my finding out whether or not I am angry: it is neither more nor less odd to speak of my finding out whether or not I am anger behaving.

3. It is not always odd to speak of my finding out whether or not I am behaving in a certain way. Suppose I have my hands behind my back, my fingers intermeshed. I am asked to move the third finger of my left hand. I may not know whether or not I am in fact moving that finger. I may have to look in a mirror to find out. So it is not in every case odd to speak of my finding out whether or not I am behaving in a certain way. It does not follow that it is not sometimes odd.

I am at this moment talking, hence behaving in a certain way. It would be odd to speak of my finding out whether or not I am talking at this moment. No doubt one can think up cases in which it would not be odd to speak of my finding out whether or not I am talking. That is irrelevant. I am not talking about those cases: I am talking about this case, here and now, and here and now I cannot doubt that I am talking. (More can be said about this point, but I shall not try to say it here.)

It would generally be odd to speak of my finding out whether or not I am anger behaving, e.g. gnashing my teeth.

4. The second bad argument is more serious. It is this: If my being angry were a matter of my behaving in certain ways then you should be able to find out whether or not

156

I am angry for you can find out whether or not I am behaving in certain ways. But sometimes you cannot find out whether or not I am angry. Since you can, in principle at least, always find out whether or not I am behaving in certain ways, my being angry cannot be a matter of my behaving in certain ways. (Thus: "You feel fine!")

The mistake here is in the assumption that there is a difference between your finding out whether or not I am anger behaving and your finding out whether or not I am angry. There is no difference.

5. You cannot in fact always find out whether or not I am angry. I may be artful at concealing my anger and I may refuse to tell you. Neither can you in fact always find out whether or not I am behaving in certain ways. You cannot in fact find out whether or not I am flexing my abdominal muscles. I will not tell you and no one else can.

So what you can or cannot in fact find out is beside the point. What is not beside the point?

6. 'You can in principle if not in fact always find out whether or not I am behaving in certain ways. But you cannot even in principle always find out whether or not I am angry.' This contention will not bear scrutiny.

(I will not cavil over the locution 'you can in principle find out.' I consider it an instrument of obfuscation. Even so, I shall let it pass: I believe I can more or less grasp what is intended.)

You can in principle always find out whether or not I am angry because I can tell you. Hence you need attend only to my verbal behavior. (I assume that it would generally be odd to speak of my being mistaken about whether or not I am angry.) To suppose that you cannot in principle find out whether or not I am angry would be to suppose that I cannot in principle tell you whether or not I am angry. I find such a supposition unintelligible.

7. The preceding contention can be reformulated as

follows: 'You can in principle if not in fact always find out whether or not I am behaving in certain ways. In some cases at least, being angry does not involve verbal behavior. Let us restrict our attention to such cases. Then apart from my subsequent verbal behavior, you cannot even in principle always find out whether or not I am angry.'

As I said before, I more or less grasp what is intended by the locution 'you can in principle find out': I would not pretend I have a firm grasp. (One cannot have a firm grip on a jellyfish.) In so far as I can grasp what is intended, I am inclined to agree that apart from my subsequent verbal behavior you cannot even in principle always find out whether or not I am angry. But I deny that apart from my subsequent verbal behavior you can in principle always find out whether or not I am anger behaving.

8. Let us suppose that in a certain case my anger behavior consists, among other things, in my gnashing my teeth. If we are to suppose that apart from my subsequent verbal behavior you can in principle always find out whether or not I am anger behaving then we must suppose that apart from my subsequent verbal behavior you can in principle always find out whether or not I am gnashing my teeth.

There is a difference between my gnashing my teeth and the gnashing of my teeth. It is conceivable that by supplying the appropriate stimuli directly to the appropriate muscles one could effect the gnashing of my teeth. In the kind of case I envisage, I could not truly say 'I was gnashing my teeth' though I could truly say 'My teeth were gnashing' and perhaps add 'It felt queer.'

I would not deny that apart from my subsequent verbal behavior you can in principle always find out whether or not my teeth are gnashing. But I deny that apart from my subsequent verbal behavior you can in principle always find out whether or not I am gnashing my teeth.

9. Can a behaviorist make a distinction between my gnashing my teeth and the gnashing of my teeth? I see no reason why not.

It is true that my teeth are gnashing if and only if it is true that certain teeth and jaws are moving in certain ways. But it is true that I am gnashing my teeth if and only if it is true that a certain organism is behaving in certain ways. If a certain organism is behaving in certain ways then it may be the case that certain teeth and jaws are moving in certain ways. But the converse need not hold: it does not follow that if certain teeth and jaws are moving in certain ways then a certain organism is behaving in certain ways.

10. There is a difference between someone gnashing his teeth and the gnashing of someone's teeth. But the difference is not a difference in behavior: only the former is an instance of behavior; the latter may be a component of behavior.

If George is gnashing his teeth then George's teeth are gnashing. But whether or not a case in which his teeth are gnashing can rightly be characterized as a case in which he is gnashing his teeth depends (not on whether or not the gnashing of his teeth is accompanied by "a movement of the soul" but simply) on contextual and relational matters.

11. I said that whether or not a case in which George's teeth are gnashing can rightly be characterized as a case in which George is gnashing his teeth depends on contextual and relational matters. I am not saying 'Whether or not a case in which my teeth are gnashing can rightly be characterized by me as a case in which I am gnashing my teeth depends on contextual and relational matters': that would be odd. It would indicate that I could in general answer the following generally odd question: 'Given that your teeth are gnashing, what entitles you to say not merely that your teeth are gnashing but that you are

159

gnashing your teeth, that you are doing it?' (I believe that Wittgenstein once said "The first mistake is to ask the question": the second is to answer it.)

What is in question here is what entitles you to say that I am gnashing my teeth and not merely that my teeth are gnashing. The question whether I am gnashing my teeth or whether my teeth are merely gnashing is a question for you, not for me. It would generally be odd for me to ask 'Am I gnashing my teeth or are they merely gnashing?'

12. Whether or not a case in which my teeth are gnashing can rightly be characterized by you as a case in which I am gnashing my teeth depends on contextual and relational matters.

The teeth of a corpse may be gnashing but the corpse cannot (without oddity) be said to be gnashing its teeth. So I must be alive, I must behave in characteristic ways. What more is required? Primarily this: My subsequent behavior, both verbal and otherwise, must be consonant with the claim that I was in fact gnashing my teeth. This is not to say that if I assert 'I was not gnashing my teeth,' then I was not gnashing my teeth: I may be lying, or forgetful, or confused. But my subsequent behavior, both verbal and otherwise, is clearly relevant.

Therefore I deny that apart from my subsequent verbal behavior you can in principle always find out whether or not I am gnashing my teeth. And in consequence I deny that there is a difference between finding out whether or not I am behaving in certain ways and finding out whether or not I am angry.

Philosophical behaviorism is not a metaphysical theory: it is the denial of a metaphysical theory. Consequently, it asserts nothing.

XII

The Feelings of Robots*

COULD a robot have feelings? Some say of course.[1] Some say of course not.[2]

1. I want the right sort of robots. They must be automata and without doubt machines.

I shall assume that they are essentially computing machines, having micro-elements and whatever micro-mechanisms may be necessary for the functioning of these engineering wonders. Furthermore, I shall assume that they are powered by micro-solar batteries: instead of having lunch they will have light.

And if it is clear that our robots are without doubt machines then in all other respects they may be as much like men as you like. They may be the size of men. When clothed and masked they may be virtually indistinguishable from men in practically all respects: in appearance, in movement, in the utterances they utter, and so forth. Thus except for the masks any ordinary man would take them to

---

* Originally published in *Analysis*, XIX (1959); reprinted by permission.

[1] See D. M. MacKay, "The Epistemological Problem for Automata," *Automata Studies*, pp. 235–51.

[2] See M. Scriven, "The Mechanical Concept of Mind," *Mind*, LXII (1953), 230–240.

be ordinary men. Not suspecting they were robots nothing about them would make him suspect.

But unmasked the robots are to be seen in all their metallic lustre. What is in question here is not whether we can blur the line between a man and a machine and so attribute feelings to the machine. The question is whether we can attribute feelings to the machine and so blur the line between a man and a machine.

2. Could robots have feelings? Could they, say, feel tired, or bored?

Ex hypothesi robots are mechanisms, not organisms, not living creatures. There could be a broken-down robot but not a dead one. Only living creatures can literally have feelings.

If I say 'She feels tired' one can generally infer that what is in question is (or was or will be in the case of talk about spirits [3]) a living creature. More generally, the linguistic environment '. . . feels tired' is generally open only to expressions that refer to living creatures. Suppose you say 'The robot feels tired.' The phrase 'the robot' refers to a mechanism. Then one can infer that what is in question is not a living creature. But from the utterance of the predicative expression 'feels tired' one can infer that what is in question is a living creature. So if you are speaking literally and you say 'The robot feels tired' you imply a contradiction. Consequently one cannot literally predicate 'feels tired' of 'the robot.'

Or again: No robot will ever do everything a man can. And it does not matter how robots may be constructed or how complex and varied their movements and operations may be. Robots may calculate but they will not literally reason. Perhaps they will take things but they will not literally borrow them. They may kill but not literally murder. They may voice apologies but they will not literally

[3] I shall henceforth omit the qualification.

make any. These are actions that only persons can perform: *ex hypothesi* robots are not persons.

3. 'A dead robot' is a metaphor but 'a dead battery' is a dead metaphor: if there were a robot around it would put its metaphor to death.

What I do not want to imply I need not imply. An implication can be weakened. The sense of a word can be widened or narrowed or shifted. If one wishes to be understood then one must not go too far: that is all. Pointing to one among many paintings, I say 'Now *that* one is a *painting.*' Do I mean the others are not? Of course not. Yet the stress on 'that' is contrastive. So I say 'The robot, that mechanism, not of course a living creature but a machine, it feels tired': you cannot infer that what is in question here is a living creature.

If I say of a person 'He feels tired,' do you think I am saying that he is a living creature and only that? If I say 'The robot feels tired' I am not saying that what is in question is a living creature, but that does not mean that nothing is being said. If I say 'The robot feels tired,' the predicate 'feels tired' means whatever it usually means except that one cannot infer that what is in question is a living creature. That is the only difference.

And what has been said about 'The robot feels tired' could be said equally well about 'The robot is conscious,' 'The robot borrowed my cat,' and so forth.

4. Could robots feel tired? Could a stone feel tired? Could the number 17 feel tired? It is clear that there is no reason to believe that 17 feels tired. But that does not prove anything. A man can feel tired and there may be nothing, there need be nothing at all, that shows it. And so with a robot or a stone or the number 17.

Even so, the number 17 could not feel tired. And I say this not because or not simply because there are no reasons to suppose that 17 does feel tired but because there are good reasons not to suppose that 17 feels tired and good reasons not to suppose that 17 ever feels anything at all. Consequently it is necessary to consider whether there are any reasons for supposing that robots feel tired and whether there are good reasons for not supposing that robots ever feel anything at all.

5. Knowing George and seeing the way he looks I say he feels tired. Knowing Josef and seeing the way he looks I do not say he feels tired. Yet if you do not know either of them then to you George and Josef may look alike.

In one sense they may look alike to me too, but not in another. For George but not Josef will look tired. If you ask me to point out the difference there may be nothing relevant, there need be nothing relevant, to point to. For the relevant difference may be like that between looking at an unframed picture and looking at it framed. Only the frame here is provided by what I know about them: you cannot see what I know.

(Speaking with the robots, one can say that the way things look to me, my present output, will not be the same as yours, the way things look to you, even though at present we may both receive the same input, the same stimuli, and this is because your mechanism was not in the same initial state as mine, owing either to a difference in structure or to a difference in previous inputs.)

If we say of a person that he feels tired, we generally do so not only on the basis of what we see then and there but on the basis of what we have seen elsewhere and on the basis of how what we have seen elsewhere ties in with what we see then and there. And this is only to say that in determining whether or not a person feels tired both observational and theoretic considerations are involved and, as everywhere, are inextricably interwoven.

6. Suppose you and I visit an actor at home. He is rehearsing the role of a grief-stricken man. He ignores our presence as a grief-stricken man might. His performance is

impeccable. I know but you do not know that he is an actor and that he is rehearsing a role. You ask 'Why is he so miserable?' and I reply 'He isn't.' 'Surely,' you say, 'he is grief-stricken. Look at him! Show me what leads you to say otherwise!' and of course there may be nothing then and there to show.

So A. M. Turing posed the question whether automata could think, be conscious, have feelings, etc., in the following naïve way: what test would an automaton fail to pass? [4] D. M. MacKay has pointed out that any test for mental or any other attributes to be satisfied by the observable activity of a human being can be passed by automata.[5] And so one is invited to say what would be wrong with a robot's performance.

Nothing need be wrong with either the actor's or a robot's performance. What is wrong is that they are performances.

7. Suppose K is a robot. An ordinary man may see K and not knowing that K is a robot, the ordinary man may say 'K feels tired.' If I ask him what makes him think so, he may reply 'K worked all day digging ditches. Anyway, just look at K: if he doesn't look tired, who does?'

So K looks tired to the ordinary man. That does not prove anything. If I know K is a robot, K may not look tired to me. It is not what I see but what I know. Or it is not what I see then and there but what I have seen elsewhere. Where? In a robot psychology laboratory.

8. If I say 'The robot feels tired,' the predicate 'feels tired' means whatever it usually means except that one cannot infer that what is in question is a living creature. That is the only difference.

To speak of something living is to speak of an organism in an environment. The environment is that in which the

[4] "Computing Machinery and Intelligence," Mind, LIX (1950), 433–466.
[5] "Mentality in Machines," Aris. Soc. Supp., XXVI (1952), 61–81.

behavior of the organism takes place. Death is the dissolu-
tion of the relation between an organism and its environment. In death I am pluralized, converted from one to
many. I become my remains. I merge with my environment.

If we think of robots being put together, we can think of
them being taken apart. So in our laboratory we have taken
robots apart, we have changed and exchanged their parts,
we have changed and exchanged their programs, we have
started and stopped them, sometimes in one state, sometimes in another, we have taken away their memories, we
have made them seem to remember things that were yet
to come, and so on.

And what we find in our laboratory is this: no robot could
sensibly be said to feel anything. Why not?

9. Because there are not psychological truths about robots
but only about the human makers of robots. Because the
way a robot acts (in a specified context) depends primarily
on how we programed it to act. Because we can program a
robot to act in any way we want it to act. Because a robot
could be programed to act like a tired man when it lifted a
feather and not when it lifted a ton. Because a robot could
not mean what it said any more than a phonograph record
could mean what it said. Because we could make a robot
say anything we want it to say. Because coveting thy
neighbor's robot wife would be like coveting his car and
not like coveting his wife. Because robots are replaceable.
Because robots have no individuality. Because one can du-
plicate all the parts and have two virtually identical machines. Because one can exchange all the parts and still have
the same machines. Because one can exchange the programs
of two machines having the same structure. Because. . . .

Because no robot would act tired. Because a robot could
only act like a robot programed to act like a tired man. For
suppose some robots are programed to act like a tired man
after lifting a feather while some are so programed that they
never act like a tired man. Shall we say 'It is a queer thing

166

but some robots feel tired almost at once while others never feel tired'? Or suppose some are programed to act like a tired man after lifting something blue but not something green. Shall we say 'Some robots feel tired when they lift blue things but not when they lift green things'? And shall we conclude 'Some robots find blue things heavier than green things'? Hard work makes a man feel tired: what will make a robot act like a tired man? Perhaps hard work, or light work, or no work, or anything at all. For it will depend on the whims of the man who makes it (though these whims may be modified by whatever quirks may appear in the robot's electronic nerve network, and there may be unwanted and unforeseen consequences of an ill-conceived program). Shall we say 'There's no telling what will make a robot feel tired'? And if a robot acts like a tired man then what? Some robots may be programed to require a rest, others to require more work. Shall we say 'This robot feels tired so put it back to work'?

What if all this were someday to be done with and to human beings? What if we were someday to break down the difference between a man and his environment? Then some day we would wake and find that we are robots. But we would not wake to a mechanical paradise or even an automatic hell: for then it might not make sense to talk of human beings having feelings just as it now does not make sense to talk of robots having feelings.

A robot would behave like a robot.

XIII

The Simplicity of Other Minds*

BEING epistemically ebullient about having a mind, one wonders about others. There is the doubtful, as they say, "privilege" of "direct access" to one's own mind, but the existence of that of the therefore possibly underprivileged other is supposed to remain another matter.

This other minds is a confusion, a confluence of questions, but there are principally these: I have a mind: do I know whether others do and if I do how do I?

1. I have a mind: do others? This question is backwards; turned right it reads: Am I unlike others in having a mind?

Is the answer supposed to be difficult? That only I have a mind is nowadays not an unlikely but an at best altogether preposterous hypothesis, for altogether explicable reasons. (To suppose that a reasoned answer to this kind of question cannot be given, cannot coherently be asked for, is a curious dogma of the day.[1])

2. If only I have a mind then I am a uniquely unique being. There is nothing unique in merely being unique: identical twins apart, all of us of course are unique in that each

* Originally published in *The Journal of Philosophy*, LXII (1965); reprinted with permission of the editors.
[1] See P. F. Strawson, *Individuals*, p. 112.

of us has a different genetic constitution: we may often share opinions but rarely skin.[2] To be the only one with a mind would be another matter.

How could one conclude that one was unique in having a mind? The uniqueness of the individual with respect to skin grafts has been demonstrated over and again in the world's hospitals. Considerations in support of the conclusion that each of us (identical twins apart) has a unique genetic constitution may be adduced from various scientific disciplines and theories: from genetics, immunology, radiology.

Less than the first step in confirming the hypothesis that only I have a mind would be this: to find a conceivably relevant differential factor; unlike others, only I. . . .

3. But what if there were no relevant factor? Suppose there were an other such that he and I were not only identical twins but alike in every determinable physiological feature, we were each complete chimeras. Further suppose we behaved in virtually identical ways, displayed the same capacities, manifested the same skills, and so forth. All this could conceivably be so. Then consider the hypothesis that only I have a mind.

Could the other one and I relevantly differ only in this: I do and he does not have a mind?

4. There may seem to be various options here: yes, no, and shades between, but not really, not today.

The hallmarks of a sound theory are here, as everywhere, coherence, completeness, and simplicity: coherence is in part a matter of unity but primarily a matter of consistency, and that, given the appropriate logical legerdemain, is not here especially difficult to attain; completeness is largely a matter of filling gaps, the articulation of theory by means of supporting and subsidiary hypotheses; perhaps parsimony and completeness are the simplest available indices of sim-

[2] See P. B. Medawar, *The Uniqueness of the Individual*, pp. 186 ff.

plicity. I so gloss the obvious merely to remind you of these matters.

The question again then is: Could the other one and I relevantly differ only in this: I do and he does not have a mind? Suppose we opt for yes. Then how do we account for the fantastic state of affairs? Why do I have a mind? Why does he not have a mind? Do minds just come and go in the universe? Did one just happen to alight in my head? Is there no bait for this bird?

Say yes or even maybe and what else can one do but resolve to accept the relation, miraculous and inexplicable, between the mind and the body, anyone's of course? For it is not as though one had or is even likely to have any coherent theory of the mind in independence of the body. So there is nothing but no.

5. If no then if I am unique in having a mind then I must be unique in some further way. Of course I am: I am unlike others in that I alone have exactly the brain I have. There is certainly good reason to believe that no one ever has a brain exactly the same as anyone else's.

Shall I say that only I have a mind because only I have just the brain I do? If I argue that how shall I argue it? For why does having just the brain I do matter so much? What about my father, my mother, my children? If they do not have minds why do they not and if I do why do I?

What exactly is the difference between my brain and all others which makes such a difference? Or even roughly?

6. On the hypothesis that one is unique in having a mind, unless one has oneself been the subject of investigation, one is for the most part compelled to eschew reference to and reliance on the findings of psychologists, physiologists, biologists.

For if only I have a mind and if I have not myself been investigated, studied, examined, then though scientists may have discovered much, they are not likely to have discovered much directly concerned with the mind.

Evidently evidence is not easy to discover here. And almost anyone would soon find that the hypothesis that only he has a mind is hard to hold. And there is after all a more viable alternative.

7. I am not a uniquely unique being in being a being with a mind: others too have minds. But which? If we have minds then we have something else too. But what?

Those with a brain of course of the right sort and in the right shape. There is no problem is there of other brains? 'Are others brainless?' does not itch more than 'Are they legless?' even if it is not exactly as easy to scratch if it does. In a nut shell: There is their brain, being stimulated, responding, altogether well-behaved, exemplary, but do they have a mind? To find the mind in the brain is the rub.

To talk about the mind is primarily a fancy way of talking about mental states and mental events (themselves fancy ways of talking). There is a relation between the mind and the brain; more carefully, there are relations between mental events and neurophysiological events, between mental states and neurophysiological states. The evidence for this is today overwhelming and, on the hypothesis that I am not unique in having a mind, here available to me.

8. The futility of the hypothesis that I am unique in having a mind provides important support for the counter thesis that others too have minds. But one is not restricted here to a *via negativa*. No hypothesis that stands up under investigation, consideration, stands alone. One holds another and if they prove tenable in time all transmute from hypothesis to fact, anyway for a time. (And that childish facts continually decay in time to discarded hypotheses should prove no cause for dismay.)

To the hypothesis that my mind and my brain stand in significant relation I conjoin the hypothesis that my mind and my brain stand in this relation not because the mind is mine but because of what minds and brains are. And to these hypotheses I (as many others do) conjoin the hypothesis that among the others that have minds other animals are to be counted. (Possibly man is the only conjectural beast but one can have a mind without being remarkably speculative.) But to say that horses, dogs, rats, cats, cows all have minds is not to deny that these beings may have qualitatively radically different experiences from men.

And to these hypotheses still others must of course be conjoined. What is in force and active here then is not a silly single hypothesis that there are other minds, this naïvely supposed to be somehow based on an unexplored analogy. Instead one is confronted with a complex conceptual scheme. The fact that there are other minds is an integral part of this scheme and presently essential to it.

9. A conceptual scheme such as this, commodious enough to encompass rats and others, draws support from a multitude of observations and experiments.

The efficacy of aspirin, mescal, opium is then an eloquent testimonial to the intimate relation between mind and body, provides confirmation for each of the conjoined hypotheses of the scheme, and so participates in the baptism of the existence of other minds as a fact.

Fat rats lend their weighty support: the urgent voluntary errand of the obese overeater may be owing to hypothalamic damage:

Control of feeding behavior in the hypothalamus is located in two "feeding centers" in the lateral hypothalamus and two "satiety" centers in the ventromedial hypothalamus. Destruction of the satiety centers resulted in overeating and obesity, whereas stimulation of these centers was followed by cessation of eating. Stimulation of the "feeding centers," on the other hand, led to eating, while their destruction produced a form of anorexia so intense that afflicted animals would starve to death in cages filled with food.[3]

[3] Albert Stunkard, "Research on a Disease: Strategies in the Study Obesity," *Physiological Correlates of Psychological Disorder*, eds. Robert Roessler and Norman S. Greenfield, p. 214.

And then the experiments of other rats further bolster our familiar scheme:

There are many indications that animals in problem-box situations experiment with many solutions. Thus one rat, in experiments with the inclined-plane box (Lashley and Franz, 1919), originally opened the box by an accidental fall from the roof of the restraining cage. For several trials thereafter she systematically climbed to the roof and let go, totaling more than 50 falls before the method was abandoned.[4]

10. That there are other minds is certainly a fact of the day, but it is flaccid stuff: we live in dark ages; our slack concepts crumble, our conceptual schemes are gapped with riddles. That there is a significant relation between the mind and the brain can today hardly be doubted, but precisely what that relation is is another matter presently not known.

Current attempts to identify mental states with cerebral states, mental events with cerebral events, can only be characterized as jejune and misguided: they reveal a fundamental failure of appreciation, a failure occasioned perhaps by a profound misconception of the conceptual situation. A mental event or state is not identical with, is not one and the same thing as, a cerebral or a neurophysiological event or state. This is seen at once once one sees and appreciates the differences between the relevant principles of individuation.

11. In offering a defense of "physicalism", Quine has claimed that

If there is a case for mental events and mental states, it must be just that the positing of them, like the positing of molecules, has some indirect systematic efficacy in the development of theory. But if a certain organization of theory is achieved by thus positing distinctive mental states and events behind physical behavior, surely as much organization could be achieved

---

[4] K. S. Lashley, *Brain Mechanisms and Intelligence*, p. 135.

by positing merely certain correlative physiological states and events instead.[5]

This ploy is worth considering, though readily countered, for it serves to underline the distinctiveness of mental states and events. But first the riposte: One might as poorly argue that if the positing of molecules has some indirect systematic efficacy in the development of theory, surely as much organization could be achieved by positing merely certain correlative little objects instead. Quine adds: "The bodily states exist anyway; why add the others?" [6] Little objects exist anyway; why add mysterious little configurations?

For of course if there is a case for mental state and events then no doubt, in some sense and as Quine claims, it must be that the positing of them, like the positing of molecules, has some systematic efficacy in the development of theory. But it does not follow that the positing of states and events of another kind and character need be similarly efficacious. Obviously the positing of little objects of essentially the same kind and character as macro-objects would not only not contribute to the organization of quantum theory but would render it utterly incoherent.

What is the case for mental states and events? A minute part of it certainly is this: Our psychological concepts are important explanatory devices; one can explain someone's tendency to group certain physiologically unlike stimulations together by saying that in each case he experiences the same feeling, in each case the same mental event occurs. By so saying one can avoid saying, what anyway presently appears to be positively untrue, that in each case the same physiological event occurs.

12. Consider a particular mental event, say that which occurs when one is stung by a bee: one experiences a sudden sharp pain, perhaps of relatively short duration, say one or

[5] W. V. O. Quine, *Word and Object*, p. 264.   [6] *Ibid.*

two seconds. Can this particular mental event be identified with a particular cerebral event? Cerebral events are measured in milliseconds.

One of the big gaps in our knowledge, not filled by either physiology or by psychology, is an accurate time-space description of central nervous system electrical activity and behavior in the very short time-intervals. Psychologists tend to deal with long cumulative phenomena, the results of many billions of short-term events. The classical learning-motivation-drive studies illustrate the point; even perceptual-discrimination-motor-response experiments involve a long-term, complex, spatial-temporal sequence of stimuli of unending variety from one millisecond to the next.[7]

If, instead of particular cerebral events, one were to attempt to identify mental events with particular collections of cerebral events, the move would be somewhat more plausible but still impossible. Consider a repeatable event, say the feeling of a feather touching one's arm: one first has that feeling at one time and then again at another time, each time the very same feeling. There is no reason to suppose that exactly the same collection of cerebral events recurred.

For first it is nowadays reasonably clear that there is little reason to suppose that any sort of point-to-point relationship exists between the spot touched by the feather and a particular spot on the brain. "Stimulation of the skin at a specific spot will evoke responses in a much larger portion of the somatosensory cortex than the fraction of skin stimulated would lead one to expect on any simple point-to-point relationship."[8] Secondly, as ablation studies have shown over and over again, considerable portions of the brain may

[7] John C. Lilly, "Correlations between Neurophysiological Activity in the Cortex and Short-Term Behavior in the Monkey," *Biological and Biochemical Bases of Behavior*, eds. Harry F. Harlow and Clinton N. Woolsey, p. 84.

[8] Woolsey, p. 17.

be excised without the loss of specific functions. Thus in connection with patients who have undergone hemispherectomy, it is found that "Language, praxia and higher motor-sensory activities are usually preserved, whichever hemisphere is removed." [9] To suppose that exactly the same cerebral events recur if the same mental events recur subsequent to the hemispherectomy would seem to be a completely unwarranted supposition. More generally, any attempted identification of particular mental events with particular cerebral events, or with particular collections of cerebral events, or with particular collections of collections of cerebral events, and so forth runs afoul of the well known facts of functional plasticity: whether these be accounted for in terms of Lashley's "mass action" theory,[10] or in terms of some current version of the standard Sherringtonian picture of central nervous integration,[11] they seem effectively to exclude from serious consideration all identity theories of mind-brain relationship.

13. Mental events cannot be identified with cerebral events. But to abandon an over simple identity theory is not *ipso facto* to manufacture mysteries or substances. By the denial of identification we are not therewith saddled with multiple entities, double events. This duplicity of ontology is simply eliminable.

Any apple has of course a molecular constitution. So it has been said that:

The atomic theory is all-encompassing in the physical world; it leaves no room for micro-objects *and* correlated macro-objects; the whole point is that a macro-object is a complex microstructure and nothing more.[12]

[9] Sixto Obrador, "Nervous Integration after Hemispherectomy in Man," *Cerebral Localization and Organization*, eds. Georges Schaltenbrand and Clinton N. Woolsey, pp. 144–45.

[10] See Lashley, *op. cit.*

[11] See R. W. Sperry, "Physiological Plasticity," *Biological and Biochemical Bases of Behavior*.

[12] Richard B. Brandt, "Doubts about the Identity Theory," *Dimensions of Mind*, ed. Sidney Hook, p. 69.

Brandt adds that "There is not similar compulsion to identify stabbing pains with states of the brain." [13] On the contrary: the compulsion is quite the same and to be resisted in either case.

I hold an apple in my hand; this apple is not identical with, is not one and the same thing as, a particular collection of molecules. That cannot possibly be so: I do not lose and acquire a new apple each time I toss it in the air; yet the molecular constitution of my apple fluctuates from toss to toss: the collection constituting the apple at one toss is not identical with the collection constituting the apple at another toss. Unless the transitivity of identity is to be called into question, this is not a case of identity.

Then is my apple to be identified with a particular class of spatiotemporally ordered collections of molecules? But which collections? (Exactly how many hairs can a bald man have? Is water H^2O? A glass of lake water is not a glass of H^2O. Isn't lake water water?) And one can bite an apple but could one bite that class of spatiotemporally ordered collections of molecules? Or cut it in half? (Alternatively it is sometimes suggested that the apple is identical not with a particular collection of molecules but with a particular configuration of molecules. The switch from 'collection' to 'configuration' accomplishes nothing; the same problems remain: radically different principles of individuation are still involved.)

14. Apples can no more be identified with collections of molecules than mental events can be identified with cerebral events. But that does not mean that apples must be spiritual concomitants of collections of molecules. If there is no collection of molecules sporting in the neighborhood of a branch then there is no apple dangling there.

To class something an apple is to employ a particular form of conceptualization, to class something a collection of molecules is to employ another. These two forms of conceptualization are two, not one, but they are not totally unrelated: in

13 *Ibid.*

each case that which is conceived of is an entity of a sort. These two entities, so conceived, are neither one and the same entity nor yet exactly two different entities.

One of the simplest relations one could hope to find between entities would be that of identity: the entity conceived of as an alpha proves to be identical with, one and the same as, that conceived as a beta. Another simple relation would be that of difference: the entities conceived of are not only not the same but the existence of one is wholly independent, directly or indirectly, of the existence of the other. Between these two extremes there are innumerable cases and there one finds apples and collections of molecules, minds and brains.

15. Psychophysiology is that relatively new branch of science concerned with determining the specific relations obtaining between mind and brain. Its task is to find and state dyadic translation functions, functions that take as arguments ordered pairs, one member of which ranges over psychological matters, the other over physiological matters.[14] The function of a psychophysiological dyadic translation function is to coordinate psychological and physiological descriptions, referential expressions, and so forth, and so bridge the conceptual gap between these different forms of conceptualization.

An identity relation is a simple translation function serving to coordinate different descriptions at the same conceptual level. It is of no utility in connection with expressions exemplifying radically different forms of conceptualization. There is no reason to suppose that an identity function can be of any utility in psychophysiology: the forms of conceptualization employed there are too markedly different to allow any such easy interrelation.

16. There is a translation function that serves to coordi-

[14] See Albert F. Ax, "Psychophysiological Methodology for the Study of Schizophrenia," *Physiological Correlates of Psychological Disorder*, eds. Roessler and Greenfield.

nate our talk about apples with talk about collections and configurations of molecules. It is not a simple identity function.[15] It is complex and difficult to state. For from the point of view of macro-entities, talk about micro-entities is inevitably excessively definite, exact, precise. A particular apple is not a particular class of spatiotemporally ordered collections of molecules, and even if it were, to bite an apple would not be to bite the class but rather to segment some member(s) of the class; but of course the members of such a class, namely collections of molecules, are not specifiable.[16]

Adequate translation functions are hard to come by in psychophysiology; in fact none are known. The reasons for this remarkable lack of knowledge are largely but not exclusively technological. Ablation and stimulation are the major methods of cerebral and neurophysiological research. The presently insuperable problems posed by such techniques should be obvious: think of attempting to determine the functions of the various parts of a full scale computer by examining the computer's output after removing bits of its mechanism or tampering with its input; and this greatly understates the problem. But the present state of technology is not the only significant difficulty in providing plausible psychophysiological translation functions.

17. Without peering overmuch, one can make out an unfortunate mentalistic conceptual scheme generally accepted today. One can discern an internally structured, albeit incoherent, set of concepts. There appears to be no end to tiresome talk of intentions, of motives, of direct awarenesses. It is this scheme that gives rise to the disembodied spirit, the death survivor, the telepath, the sufferer of ghostly agonies in the fireless flames of hell. Disembodied

[15] See Hilary Putnam, "Minds and Machines," *Dimensions of Mind*, ed. Hook, pp. 155 ff. Putnam's "theoretical identification" is I believe best thought of as a relatively complex translation function.
[16] See Max Black, *Problems of Analysis*, pp. 27 ff., in connection with the nonexistence of rigidly demarcated classes.

spirits not being choice physiological subjects, it need not be a source of astonishment that adequate translation functions are not at once available for all mentalistic concepts.

But fortunately conceptual decay is the order of the day. The current mentalistic scheme is gradually giving up the ghost. Our intellectual concepts, thinking, planning, experimenting, all are tottering; intelligence looks to be not importantly different from a trait of mechanical morons with lightning-like access to prodigious memories, computers. But no doubt pain and other plain concepts are likely to survive. And possibly in time, if the race lingers on, adequate translation functions will be found for the survivors.

Bibliography
(of works referred to)

Alexander, Samuel. *Philosophical and Literary Pieces*. London: Macmillan, 1939.

Bell, Clive. *Art*. New York: Capricorn Books, 1958.

Berenson, Bernhard. *Aesthetics and History*. Garden City, New York: Doubleday, 1953.

Black, Max. *Problems of Analysis*. Ithaca: Cornell University Press, 1954.

Chomsky, Noam. *Aspects of the Theory of Syntax*. Cambridge; M.I.T. Press, 1965.

——. "On the Notion 'Rule of Grammar,'" *Structure of Language and Its Mathematical Aspects* ("Symposia in Applied Mathematics"). New York; American Mathematica Society, 1961. Pp. 6–24.

——. *Syntactic Structures*. The Hague: Mouton & Co., 1957.

Collingwood, Robin G. *The Principles of Art*. Oxford: Clarendon Press, 1955.

Cortissoz, Royal. "The Post-Impressionist Illusion," *Three Papers on "Modernist Art."* New York: American Academy of Arts and Letters, 1924. Reprinted from *Century Magazine*, April 1913.

Cox, Kenyon. "The 'Modern' Spirit in Art," *Three Papers on "Modernist Art."* New York: American Academy of Arts and Letters, 1924. Reprinted from *Century Magazine*, April 1913.

Dewey, John. *Art as Experience.* New York: Minton, Balch & Co., 1934.

Empson, William. *The Structure of Complex Words.* London: Chalto & Windus, 1951.

Fry, Roger. *French, Flemish and British Art.* New York: Coward-McCann, 1951.

——. *Vision and Design.* Baltimore: Pelican Books, 1937.

Harlow, Harry F., and Clinton N. Woolsey, eds. *Biological and Biochemical Bases of Behavior.* Madison: University of Wisconsin Press, 1958.

Hook, Sidney, ed. *Dimensions of Mind.* New York: Collier Books, 1961.

Kant, Immanuel. *Critique of Aesthetic Judgement.* Oxford: Clarendon Press, 1911.

Katz, Jerrold J., and Paul M. Postal. *An Integrated Theory of Linguistic Descriptions.* Cambridge: M.I.T. Press, 1964.

Lashley, Karl S. *Brain Mechanisms and Intelligence.* New York: Dover Publications, 1963.

MacKay, Donald M. "The Epistemological Problem for Automata," *Automata Studies.* Princeton: Princeton University Press, 1956. Pp. 235–251.

——. "Mentality in Machines," *Aristotelian Society Supplement,* XXVI (1952), 61–86.

Medawar, Peter B. *The Uniqueness of the Individual.* New York: Basic Books, 1961.

Quine, Willard V. O. *Word and Object.* New York: John Wiley & Sons, 1960.

Roessler, Robert, and Norman S. Greenfield, eds. *Physiological Correlates of Psychological Disorder.* Madison: University of Wisconsin Press, 1962.

Schaltenbrand, Georges, and Clinton N. Woolsey, eds. *Cerebral Localization and Organization.* Madison: University of Wisconsin Press, 1965.

Scriven, Michael. "The Mechanical Concept of Mind," *Mind,* LXII (1953), 230–240.

Stauffer, Robert C., ed. *Science and Civilization.* Madison: University of Wisconsin Press, 1949.

Strawson, P. F. *Individuals.* London: Methuen & Co., 1959.

Tolstoi, Leo. *What Is Art?* Oxford: Oxford University Press, 1930.

Tovey, Donald. *Essays and Lectures on Music.* New York: Oxford University Press, 1949.

Turing, Alan M. "Computing Machinery and Intelligence," *Mind*, LIX (1950), 433–466.

Ziff, Paul. *Semantic Analysis.* Ithaca: Cornell University Press, 1960.

Index

185